MULESLAI TO MUNDESLEY

Towards a History of the Village

Figure 1: The architect's drawing for Mundesley's most prominent landmark, the Grand Hotel

MULESLAI TO MUNDESLEY

Towards a History of the Village

Written by Peter Brice

Designed and illustrated by Leigh Caudwell

Assisted by Christopher West

For the people of Mundesley

MULESLAI TO MUNDESLEY

ISBN 978-1-5262-0405-9

First published 2016 by Mundesley Parish Council

© Mundesley Parish Council

This publication is available direct from Mundesley Parish Council.

Mundesley Parish Council is committed to a sustainable future for our readers and the planet. This book is made from Forest Stewardship certified paper.

http://mundesleypc.norfolkparishes.gov.uk

mundesleypcclerk@gmail.com

Printed by Cheverton Printers, Cromer.

Cover Photo: The mill pond looking towards the sea.

CONTENTS

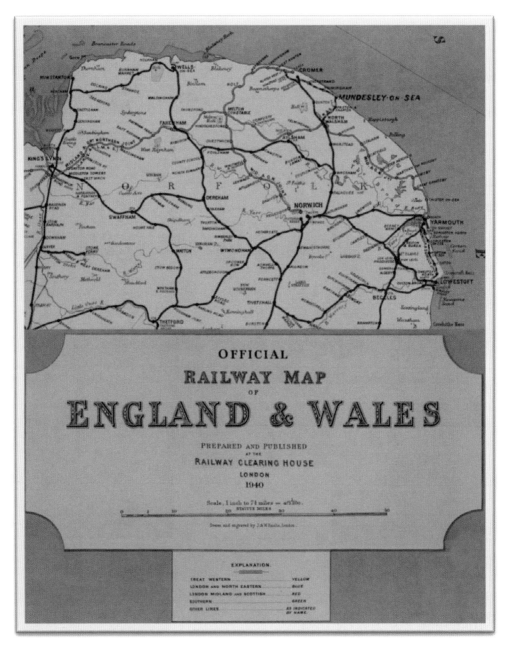

Figure 2: Mundesley's location shown on the Official Railway Map of 1940

FOREWORD

By Christopher West

Chairman of Mundesley Parish Council and of Mundesley Museum

A year ago Peter Brice came to me with some notes designed to help the stewards of the Museum and I thought they deserved a wider audience. The notes have duly become a book, and I thank Peter for his research and writing, and Leigh Caudwell for his design of the text and cover and for his many excellent photographs.

Mundesley Parish Council and Mundesley Museum are grateful to the late Charles Loades whose bequest is mainly funding the publication of  the book. Charles devoted his working life to teaching and spent his retirement in Mundesley. He threw himself into community life and became a pillar of the Mundesley establishment. He was Chairman of the Parish Council for more than sixteen years and was the prime mover in the formation of the Mundesley Maritime Museum. He was Chairman of the Horticultural Society. He was also closely involved with Coronation Hall and was perhaps best known for founding the Mundesley Festival in

1983. The Festival continues, providing summer entertainment for locals and visitors to the village.

The title *Muleslai to Mundesley* was coined by the late Mike Howard of the former Estate Agency of Howard Page for a projected (but unrealised) video of heritage photos of the village, for which he asked Peter to write the script in 1995.

Mundesley's history would be the poorer without the previous work of Christabel Hoare (*A Short History of the Parish of Mundesley* 1913), E A Goodwyn (*Mundesley Past* 1979) and Eric Reading & Paul Damen (*A Mundesley Album* 1985, new edition 2010, and still in print). We have tried not to repeat photographs and drawings used by these authors. Instead, the illustrations draw attention to aspects of Mundesley that deserve closer study.

I commend *Muleslai to Mundesley* to all who want to discover more of the village's past.

INTRODUCTION

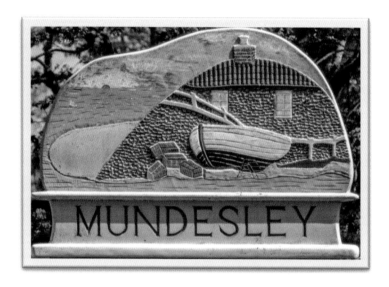

Mundesley is a small parish on the north-east Norfolk coast. It lies in the Hundred of North Erpingham, the Diocese of Norwich, the Archdeaconry of Norfolk, the Deanery of Repps, the Erpingham Rural District (1894-1974) and the District of North Norfolk (since 1974). In 1914 the parish contained 599 acres of land and 146 acres of foreshore, an acreage that is being diminished by the sea's continual erosion of the cliffs. Much of the original settlement nestles between the East and West Cliffs in the valley of the River Mun, more commonly known as Mundesley Beck. The surrounding landscape is designated an Area of Outstanding Natural Beauty. The village enjoyed its heyday as a seaside resort in the first half of the twentieth century, but it has a long and varied past, which deserves to be more widely known.

What's in a name?

The derivation of the name Mundesley is uncertain. If the name were Old English (Anglo-Saxon), it might mean *the clearing in the wood by the river Mun* but the Norfolk Historic Environment Record claims that its origin is *Mundel's clearing* in Old English, quoting J Rye *A Popular Guide to Norfolk Placenames* (Larks Press 1991). D Mills *A Dictionary of English Placenames* (OUP 2011) puts *Mul's clearing* before Mundel's, which makes sense because the *Little Domesday Book* of 1086 calls the village *Muleslai. Muleslai* becomes *Moneslee* in the Register of William Bateman, Bishop of Norwich 1344-55; *Mounsley* on Saxton's Map of Norfolk of 1579; and both *Mundesley* and *Munsley* on Faden's Map of Norfolk of 1797.

Figure 3: The pelvic bone of a southern mammoth- size 53 cm by 45 cm

1. THE GEOLOGY OF MUNDESLEY

Mundesley's cliffs stand some thirty metres above sea level at their highest points. They were created towards the end of the geological period known as the Pleistocene, which dates from 2,600,000 to 12,000 years ago. During a series of ice ages from about 300,000 years ago glaciers formed the cliffs from unconsolidated sands, gravels and clays. The cliffs are unstable. At high tide the sea undermines them, causing unconsolidated material to slump down onto the beach to be washed away by longshore drift. Springs and seepages that flow through the cliffs towards the sea also cause slumps. The coast has been in retreat for centuries: the Roman coastline probably lay two miles further out. Global warming is now accelerating the erosion: witness the emergence of the huge bay at Happisburgh since the late 1990s. Erosion means that geological items that started on the land often end up on the beach.

Mundesley Museum, opened in the Watch Tower on the sea-front in 1995 (hereafter the Museum), has a small but fairly representative collection of local fossils. The earliest, dating from some 160,000,000 years ago, is part of the flipper bone of a plesiosaur, an aquatic dinosaur. The star of the collection is the fossilised pelvic bone from a southern mammoth (*Mammuthus Meridionalis*), found on the beach by Joy

Gowing in 2006. It dates from 1,500,000 to 2,500,000 years ago. A femur from the same species was found in Mundesley in 1920: the Museum has a press picture showing it with the pioneer Norfolk geologist Frederic William Harmer (1835-1923) when he was 85. Also featured are a mammoth's tooth and the head of the femur of a young mammoth. Other large animals roamed Norfolk: the Museum displays part of a tibia of a bison or hippopotamus.

The glaciers carried fossils, rocks and minerals before them and the beach offers up a wide variety of treasures: belemnites (fossil squids); echinoids (fossil sea urchins); fossilised wood and bone; almost spherical glaciated pebbles; a rare piece of augite that may have come from Norway; agates, green jasper, or even amber; and much more.

Figure 4: The semi-polished prehistoric axehead - 14.5 cm long

2. THE ARCHAEOLOGY OF MUNDESLEY

There have been no formal archaeological excavations in Mundesley to date but many finds have been recorded in the on-line Norfolk Historic Environment Record (hereafter NHER). The erosion of the coast means that any early seaside settlements will have disappeared and that artefacts once on the land are commonly found on the beach.

Many of the Stone Age flint artefacts are not of great significance (NHER 6859, 6863, 6865, 6871, 6874, 39248, 41583), but some are exciting: a Mesolithic flint pick (NHER 6861) discovered on the beach in 1958; a Neolithic flint leaf-shaped arrowhead (NHER 6862) unearthed at 16 Beckmeadow Way in 1971; a Neolithic flint chipped axehead (NHER 6864) picked up on the beach in 1956; and a later prehistoric flint bifacial knife (NHER 39495) in 1999. A semi-polished axehead, found by Peter Corrigan, is displayed in the Museum. The Bronze Age finds are interesting: a copper alloy socketed axe (NHER 6866) found in 1933; an early flanged axehead (NHER 6867) found in c.1900; a copper alloy axehead (NHER 6868) picked up after a cliff fall in 1879; and an early stone battle-axe (NHER 18374) discovered at White House Farm in 1981. On their own these prehistoric finds suggest some pre-Roman activity in the parish, but probably not much settlement.

However aerial photography does indicate some settlement with possible evidence of burial mounds or roundhouses and of field systems, but the dating of them is uncertain. In 2004 a crop-mark (NHER 39063) was identified on the golf course: it might be a ring ditch round a Bronze Age barrow or a Bronze or Iron Age roundhouse, or perhaps a more modern feature like a ditch round a post-mill. It may be associated with other ring ditches (NHER 12805, 39064) to its north-west or with areas of multi-phase field boundaries to its north-east (NHER 39068) or north-west (NHER 39065, 38933). Aerial photography has also identified traces of post-medieval field systems (NHER 39059) which overlie earlier crop-marks of a fragmentary field system (NHER 36762) and two rectilinear enclosures (NHER 39058): these earlier crop-marks may have an Iron Age or Roman origin.

The alignment of some modern roads has led some to suggest a possible Roman road from Cawston to Mundesley via Bacton (NHER 41037), but the evidence is not strong. Any Roman settlement that might have been its coastal terminus would have been lost to the sea long ago. The Roman finds within the present parish are few: a copper alloy vessel or military camp-kettle (NHER 6869) unearthed before 1900 in the railway cutting near the church; a didrachm (coin) of Severus Alexander and Probus (NHER 6870) found on the beach in 1942; a half follis (coin) of Constantine I (NHER 23762) picked up on the beach in 1987; and some unspecified coins of Roman date (NHER 6872) discovered close to some

Anglo-Saxon cremation urns.

In 1965 building works exposed nine Early Saxon cremation urns (NHER 6872) from the sixth century. One complete urn contained cremated bone, fused glass and a bone bead. This find suggests a cremation cemetery of uncertain extent

Figure 5: A sixth century Saxon burial urn - 18 cm tall

and thus a probable settlement. The Museum displays a sixth century burial urn which appears to be one of the nine. Other Early Saxon finds include two brooches (NHER 15974, 21434) and - from Ingleside - an iron spearhead and a fragment of a shield boss (NHER 16294). The entries for Mundesley in the *Little Domesday Book* are evidence of a small Late Saxon settlement, which may have had its roots in an earlier period.

Even though there was a small, active settlement in Mundesley in the

Middle Ages, medieval finds are relatively rare: sherds of pottery and part of a green-glazed pierced strap handle found north of the parish church date from the twelfth or thirteenth century (NHER 6873); a rim sherd of hard grey pottery discovered at the foot of the cliff in 1977 is probably medieval (NHER 12543); and a base sherd picked up on the beach in 1983 belongs to the thirteenth century (NHER 19221). Medieval coin finds include a half noble of Edward III from the Treaty Series of 1363-69 (NHER 20918) uncovered as the foundations of 48 Gorse Close were dug in 1984. Two finds emphasise the importance of religious faith in the Middle Ages. The first is a lead mortuary crucifix (NHER 28516). The second is part of the body of an *ampulla* (NHER 18891), a small lead vessel used by a pilgrim to carry holy water back from a shrine - or even a drop of the Virgin's 'milk' if he or she had visited the Augustinian shrine of Our Lady of Walsingham. Mundesley was on well-trodden pilgrim routes. The parish church of Trimingham, dedicated to St John the Baptist's Head, possessed a life-sized image of the head carved in alabaster, which was revered by pilgrims: a similar image survives in the Victoria and Albert Museum. At the Cluniac Priory of Bromholm at Bacton pilgrims venerated a fragment of the 'true cross' acquired by the monks in 1223: the story of the fragment is told by the chronicler Matthew Paris (c.1200-59); and the *'rood of Bromholm'* features in Langland's *Piers Plowman* and Chaucer's *Canterbury Tales*.

3. DOMESDAY MUNDESLEY

Like many places in Norfolk, the written history of Mundesley begins with the *Domesday Book*, a thorough survey of England made in 1086 by William the Conqueror to help him meet the threat of invasion posed by his rebellious son Duke Robert of Normandy and King Cnut of Denmark. The survey was probably not intended to assess the country's wealth for tax purposes, because the organisation of the *Domesday Book* makes it a clumsy tool for collecting tax. More probably the king intended to assert political control over his tenants-in-chief and those who depended on them in the feudal system - that descending pyramid of land in return for service, military or agricultural. Commissioners went round each county in 1086 asking questions about each landholding or manor in the time of King Edward the Confessor (1042-66) and again in 1086. The answers collected from most counties were edited and written into the *Domesday Book*. The unedited answers for Norfolk, Suffolk and Essex were bound into the separate *Little Domesday Book*.

The entries relating to Mundesley - then called Muleslai - are part of the description of the lands held by the Norman Earl William de Warenne, who fought at the Battle of Hastings in 1066 and who became the Earl of Surrey shortly before his death in 1088. His principal Norfolk holding was at Castle Acre but he also held the Soke of Gimingham (see below). In Mundesley his manor stretched from the Beck to Lood (or Loos) Yard and he held rights over the wreck of the sea and all royal fishes. The two Muleslai entries read:

A free man called Grimketel [probably of Norse or Danish origin] *holds 30 acres of land with two bordars* [unfree smallholders of no more than five acres] *and one plough* [with its team of up to eight oxen depending on the soil]. *Further William* [de Warenne] *holds in the same place 3 freemen, of Edric's TRE* [in the time of King Edward - that is, before 1066] *[with] 10 acres and one plough. It has always paid 4s* [for the geld or tax]. *[There is] 1 church with 12 acres.*

In Muselai and in Truchet [Trunch] *R[obert] Malet claims 19 free men, 3 in patronage and the others with all customary dues.*

The modern editor of the *Domesday Book: Norfolk* comments that the second entry does not make much sense. Robert Malet, Lord of Eye in Suffolk, was another great Norman landowner, and there may have been some dispute or confusion. The first entry also seems rather deficient: there are not enough lands, for the manor(s) may have comprised some 600 acres to judge by the size of the modern parish. This may be explained by the fact that Mundesley was bound up with the Soke of Gimingham. In the Danelaw (those parts of northern and eastern England that were conquered by the Danes, but were later reconquered by the Anglo-Saxons) a *soke* was a dependent but free territory scattered over several villages, in which *sokemen* or free tenants held land but still owed some obligations to the lord. In 1288 a Crown plea roll refers to *'all the free tenants in the Soke of Gimingham, in which is contained the eight villages of Gymingham, Knapton, Monesle, Southrepps, Sidestrand, Trunch, Northrepps and Trimmingham.'* The *Little Domesday Book* records that Gimingham was held in 1066 by a free man called Rathi as two carucates of land [a *carucate* or ploughland was a measure of arable land in the former Danelaw, akin to the Anglo-Saxon hide and likewise related to tax; it represented the area which a plough team of eight oxen could plough in one season, notionally 120 acres]. The *Little Domesday Book* lists Gimingham's population as 12 villeins [unfree peasants or serfs who held up to 30 acres], 40 bordars, 2 slaves and 23 sokemen, 77 in all. Northrepps, Southrepps, Trunch, Sidestrand and Mundesley together list only 68 people and no sokemen, so that all their sokemen seem to have been entered under Gimingham. The Soke of Gimingham functioned as an economic and judicial unit throughout the Middle Ages, retaining some jurisdiction over Mundesley. For example in 1496 John Russell, the Rector of Mundesley, was brought before its court for hare-coursing on the estates of the Duchy of Lancaster: clergy were forbidden to hunt by an act of Richard II. His case was referred to the King's Council (the crown then held the Duchy): he may have been pardoned. And in 1497 the court of the Soke sat with a Mundesley jury to try the case of Clement Beter who had failed to repair the highway leading to his land at *Brodsloth* in Mundesley.

The last Earl de Warenne died in 1347. His estates passed to Earl Thomas of Lancaster and then to his two daughters, Maud and Blanch. Maud married the Duke of Zealand and died childless. Blanch married John of Gaunt, Duke of Lancaster, and the former de Warenne estates, including Mundesley, became part of the Duchy of Lancaster. John of Gaunt was unpopular and his manors were targeted in the Great Revolt of 1381, but no incident was then recorded in Mundesley. The manor passed into royal ownership when John of Gaunt's son seized the crown in 1399 as Henry IV. In 1836 the Manor of Gimingham-Lancaster, including Mundesley, was held of the Crown by Lord Suffield.

In the Middle Ages other landholdings in Mundesley included the manor of the *Spriggi* or Spriggs family, held of the Earl de Warenne. This holding, like so many in the Middle Ages, had a complex afterlife, as Christabel Hoare (1913) testifies. The name Spriggy appears in subsidy rolls in 1 and 6 Edward III (1327 and 1332), but by August 1477 the Spriggy manor was held by the Paston family. In the Gimingham court rolls of 21 Henry VIII (1529-30) Sir William Paston was cited for not cleansing the beck between Mundesley and Gimingham.

4. MUNDESLEY'S CHURCH AND CHAPELS

The medieval Church of All Saints

Figure 6: This oblique aerial view of All Saints from the south east shows its nearness to the cliff

The oldest surviving building in Mundesley is the parish church of All Saints (NHER 6884), which occupies a dramatic site on the West Cliff. The *Little Domesday Book* of 1086 mentions a church with twelve acres of land. This indicates that there was a Saxon church, perhaps originally built of wood but later rebuilt in stone by the Normans. Of this early church little remains. A fragment of Norman billet moulding is built into

Figure 7: A fragment of Norman billet moulding

the nave wall to the left of the north door, and a portion of a Norman doorway survives at the north end of the nave's west wall. A Norman or Transitional archway sits at gallery level in the nave's north wall. The lancet window within the archway may be Early English and it opens on the outside near the buttress at the west end of the north wall. What happened to this early church? Was it nearer the cliff and so fell victim to

Figure 8: The Norman or Transitional arch for the lancet window

Figure 9: One of the two medieval carved heads

the erosion of the sea? Or was it largely demolished as its medieval replacement was built? Out with the old and in with the new was often the policy of medieval masons and their patrons. Whatever, the medieval church was built on high ground at some distance from the cliff edge. It dates from the fourteenth and fifteenth century, but the building restored in the early twentieth century retains few unaltered medieval features. The chancel arch shows where the medieval rood beam was once inserted, and the remains of the stairway up to the rood loft were evident in the north-east corner of the nave until the Royal British Legion screen was erected in 1949. Two medieval carvings of faces, probably corbels, have been inserted out of position in the nave wall to the left of the north door. A westward-facing niche south of the chancel arch probably housed the image of the saint to whom a nave altar was dedicated perhaps the patron saint of one of the three medieval religious guilds, those of All Saints, St Nicholas and St Mary. An image of the Virgin Mary may have stood there, as now, because in the later Middle Ages the Lady Altar was often sited to the south of the chancel.

Figure 10: The mass dial

Nearby in the south wall is a medieval piscina where the chalice and paten would have been washed during the mass. Inside close to the south door is a holy water stoup. Outside on the first buttress east of the south porch is a mass dial, now lacking the metal gnomon from its centre: its shadow would have shown when it was time for the mass. The plain octagonal font dates from the fourteenth century: it was moved from its untypical position near the north door when the church interior was rearranged in 1948. Around 1700 Peter le Neve mentions five tombstones in the church floor with indents for memorial brasses: they were probably removed during the Reformation.

We know from the *Norwich Domesday*, an episcopal survey of benefices in the Norwich diocese in the later fourteenth century, that *'the Rector hath a competent House and Scite* [site] *containing one acre and 30 perch by the King's Standard and 12 acres of land. It* [the glebe land?] *is valued at 15 marks per annum* [£10] *and at Easter 4d ob* [oblation or offering]. *Peter's Pence 13d.'* Peter's Pence was a payment of 1d per hearth made to the pope since Saxon times. By the later Middle Ages the assessment had fossilised: it is hard to imagine that there were only thirteen hearths in medieval Mundesley. The rectory was probably north of the church, for the medieval priest's door into the chancel was - unusually - in the north wall. The site of the medieval rectory, like much of the glebe, fell victim to coastal erosion long ago.

An ecclesiastical tax book of 1428 shows that Mundesley paid 4s.11½d a year to the Abbey of St Benet-at-Holme, near Ludham, and 14s.1d a year to the Priory of Bromholm in Bacton. It is not clear on what basis these payments were made, but Bromholm Priory held *'a mill in Monesle'* granted by its founder William de Glanvill in 1113.

All Saints in the Reformation

The government of Edward VI (1547-53) outlawed the medieval mass, imposed Protestant worship according to the *Book of Common Prayer* of 1549 (revised in 1552), and sent commissioners to every parish to list and confiscate the liturgical goods used to celebrate the mass. Compared with many Norfolk churches, All Saints was poor, as this short inventory (in modernised English) shows:

This inventory indented made the 2nd day of September in the 6th year of the reign of our most dread sovereign lord Edward the Sixth [1552]... *between William Fermor, John Robsert and Christopher Heydon, knights, and Robert Barney, Osbert Mountfort and John Calibut, esquires, commissioners ... by virtue of the King's Majesty's commission to them directed for the survey of the church goods in Norfolk, on the one part; and Nicholas Pratte and William Isokke, church wardens there, Robert Beter and Nicholas Aleyn, parishioners of the said town, on the other part. Witnesses that there remains in the custody of the said church wardens ... these parcels of goods under written:*

In primis [first of all], *one chalice with a paten of silver, weighing by estimation 8 ounces, at 3s.8d the ounce - summa* [total] *29s.8d.*
Item, one vestment of white silk [usually the whole suit of vestments worn by the priest, deacon and subdeacon at mass] *and one cope of white silk* [an outer cape worn by the priest at mass and at some other services], *valued at 6s.8d.*
Item, one old cope of red satin and one old cope of fustian [a twilled linen fabric], *valued at 3s.4d.*
Item, 2 bells weighing by estimation 9c [hundredweight], *the one 4c and the other 5c, valued at 15s the c - summa £6.15s.*

Item, 1 bell clapper, valued at 2s.

Whereof is assigned to be occupied and used in the administration of Divine Service there the said chalice and the bell weighing 4c.

In witness whereof the said commissioners and the other said persons to the inventory have put their hands the day and year above-said.

In 1517 William Harmer had left four marks to buy a vestment for the church, that is £2.13s.4d (a mark was 13s.4d). So was his vestment the one of white silk, the only one mentioned in 1552? Or had some of the liturgical goods been hidden away, lest the mass should return, as many hoped? The chalice was probably exchanged for a communion cup in the reign of Elizabeth, as often happened, though the present communion cup seems to date from about 1650: it bears the unidentified mark of three dolphins' heads. The paten of parcel gilt does not match it and bears an assay mark of 1567. Despite the church's relative poverty, the Rector James Matchet made a return of eighty-five communicants in 1603. Such returns included those aged sixteen or above in an age when half the population was probably under twenty. So eighty-five was a good number for a village where the population reached only 204 by 1801.

All Saints in decline

That All Saints remained poor is suggested by the decline of its fabric, despite the 13s.4d left by Rector John Russell in 1520 and the repair of the font ordered by the will of Sir Edmund Peck of Mundesley in 1546. The medieval tower, attached to the north-west end of the nave, collapsed in the early seventeenth century, possibly in the great storm in 1604 that destroyed Eccles Church but left its tower standing. This may account for the old saying that links the two churches *'Eccles Tower and Mundesley Church went a-courting'* (Eccles church tower, then in the dunes, finally collapsed in a great storm in 1895).

In 1741, the Rector Edward Bilstone petitioned Bishop Edward Stanley of Norwich about the repair of the nave roof, which was expected to cost £100. The roof was *'so broken down and decayed that the congregation could not without danger assemble therein.'* A faculty was granted, permitting the sale of two of the three bells hanging in a separate bell-frame in the churchyard. These three bells are first mentioned by Peter le Neve around 1700 but only one bell was left in 1552 by Edward VI's commissioners: when had the other two arrived? The proceeds from the sale together with funds raised by the parishioners paid to re-roof the nave and re-hang the largest bell, which had been cast by William Brend of Norwich in 1599. However, on 1 January 1779 a great storm blew off most of the nave roof, *'the chancel having been roofless for upwards of*

20 years.' The solution adopted was to shorten the nave by twenty-three feet; to reduce the height of its walls by six feet; to erect a tiled pyramid-shaped roof over the nave with a plaster ceiling beneath; and to add a small chancel. Thus *'the little church within the Church'* was created at a cost of £124, to which the sale of the old lead contributed £72. The earliest surviving drawings and photographs of the church show this structure, and a brass plaque on the north wall shows the extent of the church between 1779 and 1903: it was indeed a little church.

Figure 11: The brass plaque on the north wall

In 1820 All Saints' few possessions were listed as *'two pewter flagons, one silver cup with a gilt cover, proper cloths and cushions for the church, one large Bible, two Common Prayer Books, and one bell.'* Henry VIII required every church to have a Bible in English, and after 1549 two Prayer Books were needed, one for the Rector who read the services and one for the Clerk who made the responses. In the same year a terrier (a list of church lands) states there was no parsonage and lists fewer than the twelve acres mentioned in the *Little Domesday Book*. These acres were widely scattered in small parcels of land. A terrier of 1834 says that three acres and one rood had by then been lost to the sea. The losses increased and little land remained by 1908, when a terrier lists just under two acres in five parcels of land. In 1923 the last three parcels were sold to the Golf Club at £50 per acre for the extension of the course to eighteen holes in 1924. The tithe map of 1838 shows the church at least a hundred yards from the cliff, but by 1950 the Rector, John Gedge, was so concerned that continued erosion threatened the church's survival that he petitioned the king as patron to urge the local authorities to defend the base of the cliff.

One piece of land was called Sermon Acre: presumably it had been left to finance a sermon or sermons at the church, quite possibly in the early seventeenth century. In 1811 it was recorded that Sermon Acre used to provide an annual payment of 10s.6d for the poor of Mundesley, though this had been stopped for some years. However, when a few years later the Acre was sold to William Barcham, he was obliged to pay the 10s.6d a year for the poor, to which other funds were added so that the overseers could offer bread, clothing or coal to the poorest in the parish.

The Church and the Chapels in the Religious Census of 1851

The Religious Census of 1851 reported the attendances at All Saints as 50 adults and 17 Sunday scholars in the morning of 30 March and 97 adults and 17 scholars in the afternoon. Counting attendances, not people, made for confusion, since one person could attend two or more services. In an imaginary village with 100 inhabitants, the rector counted 60 attendances: Horace Mann, who analysed the figures, recorded this as an attendance of 60%. However there were two services to which 20 people went twice and 20 only once, so that only 40 worshippers made the 60 attendances. To turn attendances into worshippers, Mann counted morning attendances as if they were all worshippers, and added half the attendances in the afternoon and a third in the evening. Thus Mann's figures for All Saints would be $50 + 48 = 98$ adults and $17 + 9 = 26$ scholars. Nonconformists objected as their main service was usually in the afternoon or evening. So today's historians normally add the attendances at the best attended service to one third of the attendances at any other service(s). That favours Mundesley's Anglicans, because their best attended service was in the afternoon: the worshippers in All Saints would be calculated as $97 + 17$ from the afternoon and $17 + 6$ from the morning, a total of 114 adults and 23 scholars. Even so, these figures were still below average for Norfolk and compared unfavourably with the Nonconformists.

Figure 12: The British Schoolroom where the Wesleyans and Primitives worshipped in 1851

The Mission Chapel (now the Free Church), built in 1843, was described in the Census as *'Nonconformist but not denominational.'* It reported 89 attendances in the afternoon of 30 March 1851 and 58 in the evening, which modern calculations count as 108 worshippers. The Wesleyan and Primitive Methodists both met in the British School Room, built in 1835 or 1836. The Wesleyans recorded 27 attendances in the morning and 91 in the afternoon, suggesting 100 worshippers in all. The Primitives reported 80 attendances at their one service in the evening. So altogether the Nonconformists recorded 345 attendances, representing 288 worshippers and outnumbering the Anglicans. As the population was 451 in 1851, most Mundesley people worshipped on Census Sunday: 137

Anglicans, 100 Wesleyans, 80 Primitives and 108 at the Mission Chapel - a total of 425! However, these figures hide the fact that worshippers commonly crossed denominational boundaries. As late as 1851 some Wesleyans still attended their parish church, and some Primitives probably swelled the afternoon congregation at the Mission Chapel. Even so the numbers at the afternoon services across the denominations are impressive: 97 + 17 at All Saints, 89 at the Mission Chapel, and 91 at the Wesleyan Chapel - some 294 worshippers and almost 65% of the population.

As the population of Mundesley had more than doubled from 204 in 1801 to 454 in 1841, Anglicans knew - even before the Religious Census - that the Nonconformists were attracting higher numbers than their own. So they created more seats in All Saints in 1844, a common - if ill-advised - denominational response to competition. All Saints obtained a grant from the Incorporated Society for Promoting the Enlargement, Building and Repair of Churches to build a tiered gallery at the west end of the nave with a small extension to provide access, create a clergy vestry and house the bell. The outer doorway of the south porch was partially infilled to match the doorway of the new western extension. The south door into the nave was filled in and a smaller doorway created to allow for the width of the new gallery. The gallery increased the number of free seats by 119 to the 139 reported in the Census of 1851, when 180 seats were still subject to pew rents (pew rents faded away in the later nineteenth century). The arms painted on the front of the gallery are those of Victoria (1837-1901), flanked by those of England on the left and those of the Bishop and See of Norwich on the right. All Saints rallied somewhat in the second half of the century. In 1853 public subscription purchased an organ, probably the first, which was housed in the gallery. In 1891 a new rectory, designed by Herbert Green, was built on a one acre site on Paston Road at a cost of £1500, *'provided by private benefaction supplemented by a free grant from Queen Anne's Bounty of £600.'* And in the 1890s gifts of liturgical goods to the church began to increase.

Figure 13: The arms of Queen Victoria

All Saints restored and refurbished in the early twentieth century

Even so, when the Rev Thomas Tegg Harvey became the Rector in 1896, he found that the church was in dire need of repair and restoration, a work he led with energy and determination. A plan was made to rebuild the church on what is now Gold Park on a site worth £450 offered by the East Coast Estates Company, but by mid 1902 the New Church Building Fund stood at only £1,280. So the plan was abandoned, and with the consent of the donors the Fund became the Old Church Enlargement Fund. Work advised by the Diocesan architect Arthur J Lacey and sensitively carried out by the local builder Sidney Arthur Randall saw the pyramid roof removed, the nave extended to its original length, a third of the original chancel restored and the whole church re-roofed. The nave's north doorway was opened up and a new door was fitted. A new organ chamber was constructed to the north of the nave and a new organ was purchased for £400 in 1904 to replace the one bought in 1853. A new oak holy table and communion rails were installed and the old reredos was adapted to fit. The windows in the nave and chancel were reconstructed using some of the original tracery found in the churchyard: most are in a style that we might call 'restored' Perpendicular, but the one with Y-shaped tracery follows an earlier style. Similar discoveries enabled the rebuilding of the chancel arch. New radiators were heated by a boiler sited in a basement beneath the organ chamber. These works were completed at a cost of £1,973.0s.4d, raised by public subscription, by church collections and by sales of work, fetes and the like. The church was rededicated by Bishop Bertram Pollock of Norwich on 16 August 1903.

The seating consisted of the old pews and rows of chairs. The latter were replaced in 1908 by twelve new matching pews. In the same year the old pendant oil lamps gave way to gas-lit chandeliers: town gas had been manufactured in the village since 1903. A gas-powered pump was also used to pump the organ until 1934 when an electric pump was installed. In 1910 a choir vestry, costing £150.16s.8d, was built on the foundations of the fallen medieval tower.

Figure 14: The Norman & Beard organ

The restoration of the chancel was completed in 1914. The priest's door was moved from the north wall to the south to accommodate a new organ chamber, where a fine Norman & Beard organ replaced the much inferior organ of 1904. The new organ was the pride and joy of the organist, Mr A R Steward (1903-29, 1946-53): it was thoroughly overhauled in 1952. The chancel was rededicated by Bishop Bertram Pollock on 16 June

1914. In the same year the oak lectern was purchased and the two prayer desks were presented, one by Lady Christabel Hoare of Sidestrand Hall, the other in memory of Henry Fielder Johnson of Mundesley House. The choir frontals were given later in memory of the Rev Thomas Tegg Harvey by his family.

The Rev Samuel Frederick Leighton Green worked hard to beautify the church. Public

Figure 16: The logo of the designer W E Tower from the bottom left hand corner

subscription and a profitable bazaar raised £400 to instal the east window in 1923. It was the work of an Arts and Crafts Movement designer, W E Tower, who was also responsible for the

Figure 15: The Pedder Memorial Window

Pedder Memorial Window of 1924 in the nave's south wall. The Pedder window includes Tower's logo, which adds a tower to the wheat-sheaf emblem of his associate C E Kempe. The window commemorates Arthur Edward Pedder who died on 5 February 1916, Edward Boynton Pedder killed in action on 17 January 1916, and Evelyn Mary Pedder who died on 25 December 1918. The Rev S F Leighton Green also led the building of the Church Rooms in 1924.

Figure 17: The mid twentieth century Virgin and Child in the medieval niche

Public subscription raised the £780 needed for the rood screen and loft, which were erected in 1929 in memory of the Revs T Tegg Harvey and S F Leighton Green, while the crucifix or rood with its flanking figures of the Virgin Mary and St John was Mrs Beville's memorial to her daughter. The whole would have appealed to the Anglo-Catholic tastes of the two Rectors. The Rev Thomas Williams-Fisher so disapproved of the figures that he removed them in 1931 without authorisation: the Consistory Court required their replacement. The colours of the Mundesley and District Branch of the Royal British Legion were dedicated in All Saints on 17 July 1927. The Branch later created the Royal British Legion Screen across the 1903 organ chamber. Its bronze tablets bear the names of those who fell in World Wars I and II, those from World War I being moved from the north-east corner of the nave. The Jacobean Memorial Pulpit and its tester were a gift from Sprowston Parish Church. The screen and the pulpit were dedicated in 1949, when the aumbry was inserted into the sanctuary's north wall after it was found that the communion wine was mysteriously diminishing! The last Rector of Mundesley (before the Trunch Team Ministry was established under the Rev Garth Norman in 1980) was John Gedge who served from 1946 to 1979. In 1952 he established the two nave altars and set the statue of the Madonna and Child in the medieval niche.

The rectory on Paston Road was occupied by the Rev H C Casson and by the Rev Tegg Harvey until 1920, but the Rev Leighton Green preferred to rent accommodation in Goodwin Road. In 1924 the rectory was sold for £1400 and in 1931 a new rectory was created from two adjoining houses in Goodwin Road (St Edmund's and St Winifred's). Eventually the Rev John Gedge moved out of Goodwin Road into rented premises in High Street. The rectory was let and then sold, and eventually another new rectory was built in Gimingham Road.

The restored All Saints' Church is listed grade II as a building of national importance by Historic England.

All Saints' activities in the early twentieth century

Writing in December 1900, the Rev Thomas Tegg Harvey addressed his parishioners on the eve of the new century. These are some of his words: *'...Let me say one word to you who are fathers or mothers. I urge you most earnestly to realize your responsibility in the sight of God; your*

children are being influenced by you either for good or for evil. Is God's

Figure 18: The fully restored interior of All Saints

word honoured in your home? Is God's day kept holy? Do you so

arrange your households that all can get to God's house once or twice? I

thank God that so many men and elder lads do come to our old Church,

but there are so many who I know go nowhere...' He continued in similar

vein to address young men and women and then boys and girls. He

revisited the theme several times in the *All Saints' Church Monthly*

Magazine, first published on 1 January 1904 (the Museum has a bound

copy covering 1904-05). The magazine, which must have replaced an

earlier one, was mostly composed of brief notices and news but included a substantial and popular insert called *Home Words*. The notices and news point to an active church. Services were advertised and by 1914 Morning Prayer was at 11.00 am and Evening Prayer at 6.30 pm, with children's services on the second Sunday of the month but on every Sunday from early July to mid September. Holy Communion was celebrated from October to Easter on the first Sunday at 8.00 am and on the third Sunday at noon; from Easter to the end of June on the first and third Sundays at 8.00 am and on the second and fourth Sundays at midday; and from July to September every Sunday at 8.00 am, on alternate Sundays at midday, and on the fifth Sunday in the evening. Evidently the congregation was considerably increased by summer visitors, for whose children three beach services a week were provided in August 1904. They were probably organised by the inter-denominational Children's Special Service Mission (CSSM), which was certainly working in Mundesley before World War I. In the 1960s the CSSM became the Scripture Union, which restarted a beach mission in Mundesley in the 1990s.

All Saints ran regular activities for many groups: a Bible class for young men and another for young women; a Sunday school, with its annual treat and prize-giving (the Rector had a special concern for children); a choir, with an annual treat for its boys and an annual supper for its adults (the choristers were vested in cassocks and surplices for the first time when the choir vestry was dedicated by Dean Russell Wakefield of

Norwich in 1910); a confirmation class (the class of 1905 met twice weekly and seven girls and seven boys were confirmed on 29 March); a monthly service for women; the Mothers' Union, first mentioned in 1904 and very active by 1910; the hope, probably unrealised, for a branch of the Girls' Friendly Society; a monthly missionary prayer meeting; the Sowers' Band (should it be Sewers' Band?) who made items for sale to support the Church Missionary Society; the Monthly Meeting of Church Workers - principally the Sunday school teachers and the magazine distributers - to pray and plan (there was as yet no Parochial Church Council); and a reading room run during the winter with 22 attenders a night in 1903.

All Saints also held special services, lantern lectures (the lantern was lit by acetylene gas), concerts and organ recitals to raise money for good causes. Some of these causes were especially favoured by Anglicans: the Church of England Temperance Society; the Church's Mission to the Jews; the Society for the Propagation of the Gospel; the British and Foreign Bible Society (Norton T Wakelin was the Society's agent in Mundesley); the Church Pastoral Aid Society; the Colonial and Continental Church Society; the Church Army; the Medical Mission; the South American Missionary Society; Benefice Augmentation; and the Diocesan Fund. Favourite services were the Harvest Thanksgiving and the Friendly Societies' Church Parade, but one that is now rare was the service for the King's Accession Day with a prescribed liturgy from the

Book of Common Prayer. A special service was conducted on Saturday 2 February 1901, the national day of mourning for Queen Victoria, who had died on 22 January. Other causes had a wider appeal: the Norfolk & Norwich Hospital; the Fakenham Nursing Home; the Agricultural Benefit Society; and Dr Barnardo's Homes.

The magazine also reported on the Clothing Club and the Penny Bank, which aimed to encourage planning and thrift. The Clothing Club had twenty-five depositors in 1903 and paid out a bonus of 3d in the shilling on withdrawal, financed by fourteen donors. The Penny Bank paid depositors a bonus of 1d in the shilling up to 20s, financed by six donors. There was also mention of a soup kitchen, but no details. In 1903 the Sick and Poor Fund received donations of £10.6s and in 1919 Frank Gray of Australia left £52.14s.7d to the *'Minister of the Church of England, Mundesley, for the poor of the parish.'* Invested through the Charity Commission the fund is still administered by the Rector.

Figure 19: Padre Leighton Green's World War I bugle

The Rev S F Leighton Green was a High Churchman who served as a padre in World War I, winning the Military Cross twice. His letters to his parish of St Barnabas, Heigham, are published in S J McLaren (Ed) *Somewhere in Flanders* (Larks Press

2005); and the bugle which he then carried is displayed in the Museum. As Rector of Mundesley he carried on many of the activities he inherited, but All Saints' Missionary Guild was probably his creation: it supported the societies of which he would approve, the Society for the Propagation of the Gospel, the Church Missionary Society and the Universities' Mission to Central Africa. In 1927 Mrs Skipper's membership card is signed by the General Secretary, Amy S Woods, and by the Rector.

All Saints' churchyard

The lychgate was presented by Dr and Mrs Sidney Vere Pearson for the Silver Jubilee of King George V and Queen Mary in 1935.

Figure 20: The inscriptions in the lych gate

Forethought in 1928 led to the purchase of the churchyard extension for £75, though it only came into use in 1966. The old churchyard has some interesting graves. South of the church are the tombs of Francis Wheatley and of the Larter family. To the west arc those of the Revs T Tegg Harvey and S F Leighton Green, with that of the builder S A Randall. To the east are the graves of the Revs T J Williams-Fisher and J Gedge, with that of the Rev H Crozier Casson nearby. To the west and north are sixteen war graves, but only six have War Graves Commission headstones; the seventeenth, that of W G Earl, lies to the south. The war graves were refurbished by the Royal British Legion to mark the 80th anniversary of the armistice in 1918.

The patrons, rectors and curates of All Saints

The *Norwich Domesday* of the later fourteenth century (see above) also tells us that *'the Earl de Warren* [the Earl of Warenne and Surrey] *is patron.'* At that time the glebe was worth £10 a year, a figure close to the £8.9s.9d noted by Anthony Norris in his *History of North Erpingham* in the later eighteenth century and the same as the £10 recorded in the Census of 1851. The Census recorded the tithes as £170 a year, with fees averaging £1.10s. Originally tithes were a tenth of a landowner's produce paid to the rector, but under the Tithe Commutation Act of 1836 the landowners of Mundesley agreed to exchange the tithes for a rent charge based on the price of corn. The Tithe Apportionment is dated 4 October 1838 and the Tithe Map followed in 1839. In 1914 the value of the living was listed as £180 a year. The patronage of the benefice passed to the Duchy of Lancaster in the fourteenth century and with the Duchy to the Crown in 1399. The list of named rectors may not be complete in the medieval period:

1324   Alexander de Chigwelle

1344   Henry Hap, Rector of *Moneslee,* survived the Black Death of 1349 - unlike many of his clerical colleagues.

1371   Peter de Wele

1375   John de Broghton

1380   John de Dalton

1391   John Collys or Collis

1404   John Slyngesbye

1405   John Fourbour

14--?   William Erdington

1411   Alan Thame

1426   Thomas Molenes

1464   Robert Williamson, still Rector in 1468.

14--?   John Wright

1483   John Jamys, named as Rector in the patent roll for 1 Richard III.

1484   William Davyes, said to have succeeded Wright

1485   Thomas Assehowe or Assehewe

1490   William Assehowe

1493   John Russell or Rustell

1520   Nicholas Flyght, also Parish Priest of
        Yarmouth

1523   William Curties

1542   Edmund Pecke

1546   Anthony Temple, also Vicar of Saxthorpe

1554   Thomas Breteland, also Rector of Felbrigg

1563   William Pulleyn BA (Oxon), also Rector of
        Farndon, Notts.

1580   Laurence Bond BA (Oxon)

1584   James Matchet, also Rector of Trimingham,
        was *noe graduate* and very quarrelsome,
        often resorting to law over trifling issues.

1613   Robert Smith, also Rector of Paston, was
        deprived of his cure in 1636: was he a
        Puritan deprived by the Laudian Bishop
        Wren?

1636   John Novell, a supporter of Bishop Wren.

1639   John Tenison, also Rector of Topcroft, was
        ejected by Parliament in 1642 and three

parsons served before his reinstatement in 1662:

- one Gubbard who was found to be a Roman Catholic and ejected;

- Robert Bidbank, described on his now lost memorial as *'Senior Preacher of the Gospel in this town,'* died as Rector in 1661;

- Paul Amyraut BA (Oxon), who was ejected in 1662 and became pastor of an independent church at Southrepps.

1662   John Tenison returned, also as Rector of Topcroft & Braconash. He died in 1671. His son Thomas was a pupil at the Paston School and became the hardworking Archbishop of Canterbury in 1694-1715.

1674   Wormley Martin MA

1677   John Montford MA, also Master of the Paston School 1703-21

1721   Edward Bilstone BA (Oxon), also Rector of Trimingham

1756   William Clagett, also Rector of Trimingham

1775   Jeremiah Bigsby

1783	Erasmus Druery
1798	John Nedham BA
1803	Thomas Penton
1806	Edward Hulton MA, also Rector of Trimingham
1817	Robert Steele, also Rector of Trimingham
1858	Edward Thomas Scott
1884	James Alexander Crozier MA
1886	William Richard Croxton
1888	Henry Crozier Casson BA
1896	Thomas Tegg Harvey
1921	Samuel Frederick Leighton Green MC
1929	Thomas John Williams-Fisher
1946	John Gedge
1980	Garth Norman, the first Rector of the Trunch Team Ministry
1984	John Randall
1994	Peter Allan

The list shows that some rectors were pluralists, holding Mundesley at the same time as another living. Because for long periods Mundesley had no rectory, incumbents who also held a neighbouring parish could live there and travel to Mundesley as needed: Robert Steele (1817-58) was said to have stabled his horse in the ruined chancel! Other rectors lived at a greater distance: Edward Bilstone (1721-56) dwelt *'forty miles beyond London.'* Absentee rectors usually appointed stipendiary curates to serve the cure, and certificates for three Mundesley curates survive for the nineteenth century. From 1814 Rector Edward Hulton paid William Rees £50 a year and - *'there being no parsonage house in Mundesley'* - allowed him to reside in North Walsham, where he was the Usher [under-master] of the Paston School in 1810-16 and its Master in 1825-35. In 1814 he married and moved to Trunch Rectory, serving as curate there and running a private school. His pupils moved to the Paston School in 1825. He also served as Curate at Bradfield, Trimingham, Hanworth and Alby and as Vicar of Horsey, though not all at the same time! Another Usher of the Paston School, Solomon Robinson, was the Curate of Mundesley in 1770-72.

Mundesley's Nonconformist Chapels

The Mission Chapel, built in the High Street in 1843, was also known as the Union Chapel in the later nineteenth and early twentieth century. It had 120 free seats and 70 others in 1851. Although a Sunday school was not mentioned in 1851, one existed soon afterwards; and in 1892 the

Figure 21: The Mission Chapel, now the Free Church, showing 'The Schools' at the rear

chapel was extended as 'the Schools' were erected at the rear. The census return in 1851 was signed by *'William Walker, Minister, Mrs Russell's'*: Mrs Russell ran a lodging house. Around 1890 the Minister was the Rev J R Matthews, who trained at Spurgeon's College in London, a training college for evangelists, founded by the famous Baptist preacher Charles Haddon Spurgeon (1834-92): Mr Matthews, presumably a Baptist, was such a compelling preacher that he was sometimes called the Spurgeon of the East Coast. His predecessor, the Rev Henry Walter Clabburn, is listed as the Baptist Minister of the Union Chapel in 1883. His successor, the Rev George Ince, is also listed as a Baptist in 1898, and he ran a private school at 12 Katherine Villas in Manor Road. In 1912 the Baptist Minister was the Rev James H MacDonald.

The Chapel was much involved in the Bible Conferences organised by the Rev Dr George Campbell Morgan (1863-1945), the famous British evangelist, who in 1899 succeeded Dwight L Moody as Director of the Northfield Bible Conference in the United States of America. Described as a Congregationalist in 1912, he bought Hill House in the High Street in 1906 and renamed it Northfield House: he was living there in 1912. He ran the Bible Conferences in a huge marquee in the grounds of Northfield until World War I, holding a Bible study each morning and a preaching service each evening. Thousands came up to the outbreak of war in 1914, but an attempt to revive the conferences in what is now Gold Park failed in 1934. Northfield House later became a rest home for the employees of the Metropolitan Gas Company. It has since been converted into flats and its former grounds are used for the bowling green.

Two Methodist congregations existed in Mundesley in the nineteenth century: the Wesleyans and the Primitives. The Register of Conventicles shows that on 26 February 1816 the Primitives applied for a licence in the name of farmer William Hastings to use his barn for religious worship for a congregation of Protestants. The Primitives moved to the house of farmer John Earl in 1819 and from 1835-36 they and the Wesleyans shared what was known by 1851 as the British Schoolroom in Back Street. It provided 100 free seats. Was it originally a meeting place for worship and then also the schoolroom, perhaps from 1844? In 1851 the Wesleyan return was signed by the Rev C Povah, the Superintendant Minister, North Walsham; the Primitive return by the Rev James Jackson, Minister, North Walsham. The Primitive congregation continued meeting in the schoolroom/chapel, which is now a garage or warehouse in Back Street (formerly Chapel Street?). They were still there in 1860 but the Ordnance Survey map of 1884 marks the chapel as Wesleyan. However the Wesleyans built a new chapel in Cromer Road for £1,100. It opened in 1898 and had seats for 250. The three largest Methodist denominations - the Wesleyans, the Primitives and the United Methodists - reunited nationally in 1932.

Figure 22: The facade of the Methodist Chapel in the late Victorian Gothic style

5. MUNDESLEY'S SCHOOLS

The schools of Mundesley emerge from obscurity in the nineteenth century, though private schools probably existed before then, perhaps run by chantry priests in the Middle Ages or by curates since.

Figure 23: The National School that became the Board School, showing the Boys' Entrance

Sunday schools, which taught the poor to read so that they could have access to the Bible, emerged in the late eighteenth century. Mundesley had an Anglican Sunday school in 1851, when the Nonconformists had no Sunday schools. One soon existed at the Union Chapel.

Public day schools might be funded by such societies as the Society for the Propagation of Christian Knowledge (SPCK) founded in 1698 or by local initiatives, but by the mid nineteenth century most were run by the voluntary religious societies. The largest was the Anglican National Society, founded in 1811: in 1851 it ran 360 of the 497 public day schools in Norfolk. The next largest voluntary society, the Nonconformist British Society, founded in 1808, had only 49: one was in Mundesley, where the British Schoolroom in Back Street occupied premises built in 1835 or 1836. Mundesley's National School on Cromer Road originated in the 1840s. NHER 55165 suggests its building of flint and white brick dates from 1840 with alterations in 1908, but the trust deed was signed and the site bought in 1848. Typically voluntary schools taught the four Rs: religion, reading, writing and arithmetic, as well as more practical skills such as needlework and perhaps cooking for girls and gardening for boys. Such schools were not free: most charged 1d or 2d a week. Three teachers are named in the 1851 census: Jane Wright, Mary Pyecraft and John Walker, but only John Walker is ascribed to a school (the British). The census also mentions Ann Withers as a former schoolmistress. Emma Phillips taught at the National School in 1854, when Rebecca Russell is also listed as a teacher at an unnamed school.

MUNDESLEYS SCHOOLS

In 1870 Forster's Education Act aimed to create a national education system that the voluntary societies would accept but also accommodated those who sought non-denominational or secular schooling. It laid down that where no efficient school already existed, a school board should be elected to provide one that offered non-denominational education. It is strange that Mundesley's National and British Schools both closed: were there too few pupils to make two schools economically viable? Whatever, the Mundesley Board School opened in the National School's former building in 1874. The numbers were not large: in 1877 headmistress Ellen True had only forty-five pupils. Miss S M Harris is listed as the mistress in 1883. School did not become compulsory until 1880, when Mundella's Act enforced attendance from five to ten - and from ten to thirteen if attendance and attainment had been unsatisfactory. So the visit of Her Majesty's Inspector to Mundesley on 21 June 1899 would have been an anxious occasion. Compulsory schooling made it almost inevitable that it should be free, as it largely was by 1891. The leaving age was raised to eleven in 1893, to twelve in 1899 and to fourteen in 1918.

In 1902 Balfour's Education Act abolished School Boards, made County and County Borough Councils into Local Education Authorities, giving them authority over all elementary schools (the old board and voluntary schools), and requiring them to provide secondary grammar schools. The grammar schools for Mundesley were the Paston School for Boys and

North Walsham High School for Girls. In Mundesley the Board School became the Council School under Norfolk Education Committee and in 1902-03 it had 115 children on roll - a tight squeeze in the old Board School building. In 1905 the new Wesleyan Chapel - or presumably its schoolroom - was leased for the infants. In 1908 a new Council School was built in Trunch Road with Edwin A Lucas as headmaster. The infants then returned to the old school on Cromer Road and their headmistress in 1912 was Miss E Barnes. In 1920 they moved to Trunch Road, though the old school, leased from the Parochial Church Council, was still used for woodwork, laundry and cookery classes. During World War II the old school housed Whitehill School whose pupils were evacuated in 1939 from Gravesend in Kent along with their teacher Mr D T Webbey. In 1978 Mundesley Middle School was built on the Trunch Road site and the 1908 building became Mundesley First School. In 1965 All Saints' Parochial Church Council let the old school on Cromer Road to Norfolk County Council for Mundesley Branch Library.

Private schools are harder to trace. In 1824 the Misses Bartram launched a School for Young Ladies in Mundesley: it moved to Yarmouth in 1850. Two other girls' schools were noted in the village in 1858. In 1883 Edward Henry Boyle ran a boarding and day school for young gentlemen. George Ince ran a school at 12 Katherine Villas (22 Manor Road) in 1898. Miss Burpitt's school was functioning in Ivy Farmhouse in 1910. Mrs Clarke opened Prospect House School in High Street in c.1920, and Mrs Huett ran a school in the Dell in the 1930s and 1940s.

In January 1899 the County Council Technical School (Norfolk Adult Education?) offered an afternoon cookery course of ten weekly sessions in the Royal Hotel. The course, costing 1s or 1d a session, was aimed at young women, but the lengthy advert complained that few young women had attended the last class on laundry work.

6. EARNING A LIVING IN MUNDESLEY

The people of Mundesley

Population figures give some idea of the economic health of a parish. Unfortunately we know little of Mundesley's population before England's first census was conducted in 1801. The Black Death reached the North Norfolk coast by the end of April 1349: it would have killed a third or more of Mundesley's inhabitants, and their numbers would not have fully recovered until at least a century later. The first census of 1801 gives a small population of 204, which more than doubled by 1851, outstripping the national rate of increase. However, when other farming communities around were growing in the boom years of the late 1840s to the mid 1870s, Mundesley's population began a slow fall. When other farming communities were declining in the agricultural depression of the late nineteenth century, Mundesley's population rose quickly after 1891 as the seaside resort began to flourish. It looks as if the upward trend in numbers was interrupted in the 1920s: the reason was the transfer of part of the parish to Knapton in 1925.

Year	Pop.	Year	Pop.
1801	204	1921	1211
1831	436	1931	990
1841	454	1951	1227
1851	451	1961	1558
1861	438	1971	1536
1871	437	1981	1766
1881	377	1991	2256
1891	411	2001	2695
1901	680	2011	2758
1911	770		

Parish registers were a legal requirement from 1538. Mundesley's survive from 1724, but even after that there are breaks in the 1740s and 1750s. The registers throw up some interesting questions. For instance in 1842 the burial register records twenty-two deaths, seventeen of them children below the age of ten: in 1832 the eight recorded deaths had included only one child. What epidemic caused so many children to die in 1842?

Farming since the Middle Ages

Mundesley's fertile loamy soil has been worked from at least as early as Saxon times, but the Mundesley entries in the *Little Domesday Book* give us almost no information about farming, apart from the existence of two plough teams. By the sixteenth and seventeenth centuries the subsidy rolls, which set out the tax assessments of individuals based on their land and/or possessions, suggest that there was no dominant landowner in the parish. In the rolls from Henry VIII to Charles II eight families keep appearing as paying tax on their land: Allen, Bradfield, Clarke, Isack, Pratt, Saul, Taylor and West. Of these *Aleyn, Isokke* and *Pratt* signed the church inventory of 1552 and were thus men of some substance.

In the eighteenth and nineteenth centuries poll lists record the votes of adult male landowners in parliamentary elections. The qualification to vote up to 1831 was the ownership of freehold land worth forty shillings a year. So everyone who features on a poll list was a landowner, however small. There were nine voters in 1714, ten in 1817, and at times in-between there were generally five or so: did some owners choose not to vote? Some of the names listed in the subsidy rolls reappear: Bradfield, Pratt, Saul and Taylor. However three new names appear in more than one election: Bartram, Wheatley and Worts. The poll lists also identify owners who lived outside the parish but used land owned within it to qualify to vote. So for example in 1714 Edward Bradfield lived in Lynn and the Rev John Mundford in North Walsham. In 1832 the franchise was extended to those who held copyhold land worth £10 a year and those who leased or rented land worth £50 a year. This may account for the jump in Mundesley's voters to seventeen in the voting register in 1832 and in the poll book in 1841. The names that appear in these two lists (all living in Mundesley unless otherwise stated) are the Rev Philip Duval Aufrere (Scarning), William Barcham, Thomas Barcham, John Clipperton, Thomas Cocks, the Rev William Gordon, Thomas Greg (Coles, Hertfordshire), William Hastings, John Howard, John Howes, Skyles Juniper, John Larter, John Thomas Mower (North Walsham), Henry Nockolds, James Russell, Robert Rust, Joseph Stannard (Norwich), Matthew Starr, the Rev Robert Steele (Rector of Mundesley 1817-58 but resident in North Walsham in 1832 and Paston in 1841), and Francis Wheatley. The Tithe Schedule of 1838 and the Tithe Map of 1839 reveal that only William Barcham, Francis Wheatley and Mary Kittmer owned over a hundred acres each, while the lesser landowners included Skyles Juniper, the Rev William Gordon, William Hastings, William Jarvis, Joseph Stannard, the executors of Thomas Ewing, and the Rev W F Wilkinson. The principal landowners in 1883 were William Thomas Mullen, John Mack of Paston Hall, and George Gordon; in 1914 John Mack, G M Silley, and the Rev Edward Gordon of the Rookery.

Landowners were not necessarily active farmers, and *White's Directory of Norfolk* names six farmers in 1836: John Earl (also carrier to

Norwich), Dennis Hasdell, [William] Hastings, John Howes, Robert Jarvis and Henry Nockolds. In 1851 the census describes eight men as farmers, giving their acreage and the number of their employees (the transcription of names is not always accurate in the Museum's copy):

Henry Atkinson	60 acres	1 man, 2 boys
Thomas Barcham	130 acres	8 men
Timothy Flint	5 acres	(he was also a thatcher)
Dennis Hasdell	8 acres	1 man
William Hastings	40 acres	2 men
Skyles Juniper	50 acres	2 men, 4 boys
John Kirk	114 acres	4 men
John Payne	125 acres	3 men

Figure 24: The west wing of Ivy Farmhouse, owned by the Juniper family in 1851

Unfortunately the farms are not identified, though the Juniper Family held Ivy Farm in High Street. At least two other houses on the High Street were farms, and fields once stretched from there to Mundesley Beck. 'The Fields' - as they were known - are now covered by the Edwardian Victoria Road and Russell Terrace and by the post-war Beckmeadow Way and Meadow Drive. Nor do we learn where William Bean was farm steward in 1851. The listed farmers employed twenty-seven labourers, but forty-two men and boys are described as farm labourers in the census. It was common for farm workers to be employed casually for particular jobs, so that three workers might compete for two jobs.

One puzzle is how the open fields that characterised medieval farming became the enclosed fields that determined the eighteenth and nineteenth century landscape. There was no enclosure act for Mundesley and we must assume that the relatively few farmers in this small parish managed to negotiate enclosure by agreement. This is suggested by the field names recorded in the Tithe Schedule of 1838 and the Tithe Map of 1839: of the seventy-six named fields, twelve have the suffix 'close' which implies an enclosure. One, King's House Close, stretched down to the Beck; another, Bacon's Close on the Trimingham boundary, was lost to the sea, along with a near neighbour, Buddell Close.

In the 1830s farmers in Mundesley faced labour unrest caused by low wages and inadequate poor relief. In the Swing Riots of 1830 a group of labourers destroyed a threshing machine that belonged to Mr Hastings of Mundesley. Animals were also often targeted, so that it is not surprising that three Mundesley farmers belonged to the North Walsham Association for the Prosecution of Horse Stealers. Under the Poor Law Amendment Act of 1834 *less eligible* poor relief (less likely to be chosen) was offered by the two workhouses of the Erpingham Poor Law Union at Erpingham and Sheringham. Entry to the workhouse was a disaster for casual workers who might thus lose their home, but the farmers who employed casual labour and who contributed most to the poor rates often preferred that outdoor relief should continue disguised as sickness relief, which was permitted, when outdoor unemployment relief was not.

Things improved for both farmers and labourers in the third quarter of the nineteenth century, when farming experienced something of a golden age, but a severe and prolonged depression afflicted agriculture from the mid 1870s. *Kelly's Directory of Norfolk* of 1912 mentions only four farmers: Walter Divers of Rookery Farm, Herbert James of Fairfield Farm, Robert Ernest Golden of Hill Farm, and Mrs Harriet Mullen. Mrs Mullen is also mentioned as a landowner, but other landowners who farmed may not have been listed as farmers. Numbers of farm labourers left the land in the late nineteenth and early twentieth century. The Board School was used for lectures, sometimes illustrated by lantern slides: at the turn of the twentieth century one lecture entitled *'Canada - the Home for English Colonists'* was aimed at unemployed farm workers.

Figure 25: The mill pond looking north-east - the mill race began to the right of the tree

Mundesley's mills played an important role in the processing of the farmers' crops. From 1113 Bromholm Priory owned a mill in Mundesley: it would have been a water mill because windmills were only introduced in England in the twelfth century and were rare until the thirteenth. It was almost certainly driven by the Beck, but its precise location and its longevity are unknown. The water mill (NHER 14144) whose site and wheel now survive in the Dell was built around 1723 and

Figure 26: The remains of the overshot waterwheel

was owned by the Howard family from the later eighteenth century and then by the Larter family from the 1830s. William Larter was the miller in 1851 and employed two men, perhaps Thomas Cooke, a journeyman miller, and William Drury, a miller's labourer. In 1912 Mrs Mary Larter is listed as the miller. The mill had two brick floors with a weather-boarded upper floor and a pantile roof when seen from the pond side, but four floors and a garret when viewed from the road side. The mill was driven by an overshot waterwheel, one of only a handful in Norfolk. The wheel had a diameter of twenty-six feet and was powered by the mill pond which was in turn fed by Mundesley Beck. The Beck rises in Northrepps, meanders through Gimingham and finds its way to the sea through the Dell. When the mill was working, it used 8,000,000 gallons of water a day. The mill ground corn from local farms but also from further afield. Maize shipped from Holland to Yarmouth was carried by wherry via the North Walsham and Dilham Canal to Swafield Staithe, from where it was collected by horse and cart. Some of the resulting flour was exported on the coal ships - until the railway replaced both the wherry and the coal ship. Larter's Mill was closed in 1953. It burned down in 1956 and was demolished in 1965. Only the millpond, the wheel and its race remain. In the 1880s, but probably before and after, the Larter family also farmed on the East Cliff and had horse-drawn vehicles for hire: as a boy in the early twentieth century Reggie Clarke cleaned their wagonette, brougham and victoria, often used for weddings and funerals.

In the nineteenth century there was enough work for Larter's Mill and for Stow Mill, which stands on the hill just out of Mundesley towards Paston and may have replaced a windmill (NHER 15431) marked on Faden's Map of 1797. Stow Mill was a four-storey tower mill built by James Gaze in 1825-27 on land first acquired by his father Thomas (1) who died in 1805. In 1827 James conveyed it to his eldest son, Thomas Pleasants Gaze (2). When Thomas (2) died in 1872, the mill was offered for sale by auction in June 1873. The prospectus, prepared by Thomas Barcham, advertised

A brick tower mill in Paston in capital repair driving two pairs of Stones with Flour Mill, Jumper and all necessary tackle and gear. Also a Steam

Mill, erected a few years since, driving two pairs of stones with the five horsepower engine and apparatus thereto belonging. Also a comfortable brick and tile Residence with Granaries, Stables, Cart Lodge and Outhouses thereto belonging. FREEHOLD. The Mill is now doing a flourishing business. Possession at Michaelmas next.

However the mill was not sold, and William, son of Thomas (2), carried on the business until his death in 1906. The mill was then purchased by Mrs Mary Ann Harper, and her cousin Thomas Livermore took a yearly tenancy of the mill from 1907. Mrs Harper died in 1928, leaving the mill to Mr Livermore, but he closed the business in 1930. The mill was restored in the later twentieth century.

Fishing

Fishing for herring, cod, lobster and crab contributed to Mundesley's economy for many centuries. A document of 1276 refers to *Monsley Hith,* and *hithe* suggests a haven or port. It is possible that before Mundesley Beck was dammed to create the mill pond, its outfall formed an inlet that provided a haven. In 1816 *The Norwich Mercury* reported on Norfolk's fisheries:

The most considerable is the catch and cure of herrings at Yarmouth, Mundesley and Cromer. These three towns employ about 150 boats, from

10 to 15 tons each, and nearly 1200 men in the fishery, eight tenths of whom are drawn from husbandry work during the season. The shore department occupies about 1700 men and from 200 to 300 women, of the latter one third are constantly at work during the entire year... Mundesley cures about 200, Cromer about 400 barrels of herring.

White's Directory of 1836 names Benjamin Hastings as a cooper and fish curer, and Mack & Earl as fish curers. In 1838 the fisheries had a poor season: a large herring fleet sailing past Mundesley was forced by a change of wind to drop anchor; then a storm forced them to slip anchor and retreat in some disarray to Yarmouth, where some were reunited with anchors rescued from Mundesley beach. In 1839 Mr Mack was declared bankrupt and his furniture, horses, donkeys, omnibus and van were sold. In 1844 it was reported that Mundesley had four large boats for catching herring and seven small vessels for catching crab, lobster and cod. In that year Benjamin Hastings was still a fish curer but in 1851 he is described only as a cooper. There were seven fishermen in 1851: John and William Dix, John Earl, William Rudram (later captain of the collier *Diligence*), Samuel Warnes, Joseph and William Withers. John Rudram was then a fish dealer. By the 1860s there were only four small vessels left, and inshore fishing became the norm. The Museum displays a few items of fishing equipment: two binnacles, a marling-spike, a sailmaker's palm and a net-mending needle.

Coastal trade

Despite the lack of a jetty, the beaching of cargo vessels was an ancient practice: the *Paston Letters* record that stone was landed in this way at Mundesley in 1425. A ship was beached stern-first at high tide. Its cargo was unloaded at low tide into broad-wheeled tumbrils and pulled up into the Dell by horses or mules. The ship was then re-floated on the next high tide. It was quite a risky procedure: a ship on the beach was vulnerable to sudden storms. Captain Francis Wheatley (1770-1848), who settled in Mundesley in the early nineteenth century, operated as a merchant, ship-owner and deputy Vice Admiral of the Coast. *White's Directory* of 1836 reports that he imported 25-30 cargoes of coal yearly as well as timber. The ships left with cargoes of flour, grain and other farm produce. Two entries in the census of 1851 make interesting reading: Sarah Kirk and Mary Ann Earl were listed as sailors' wives. Men at sea were not counted in their home port, suggesting that Mr Kirk and Mr Earl were sailors, perhaps on one of Mr Wheatley's vessels: one William Kirk is listed as a master mariner in *White's Directory* in 1854. Mr Wheatley had yards for coal and timber, and after his death in 1848 the coal trade was carried on by Lacey & Bartram and later by Juniper & Company. In the 1870s Robert Juniper owned two schooners, the *Eleanor* and the *Diligence*. The latter, captained successively by George Bean, Robert Gray and William Rudram, voyaged to Hartlepool many times in 1871-74, but was wrecked on Middleton beach in 1874. The

1851 census also lists a retired master mariner, Francis William Ducker. The beaching of coal ships continued into Edwardian times but fell victim to the railway. No sailors are listed in *Kelly's Directory* of 1883, though inshore fishing continued.

Safety at sea

The major shipping lane that passes close to the shore is made perilous by the Haisborough Sands, and the burial register of All Saints refers to many sailors who lost their lives, including:

Two men names unknown from ship 'Bird' wrecked on this coast Sunday March 31st 1822.

A man name unknown from ship 'William and Ann' wrecked on this coast Sat. Feb. 1st 1823.

A lad unknown about 12 years of age, drowned from ship 'Clopton' Oct 28th 1830.

From 1799 to 1904 the register records the burial of drowned people in 1799 (3), 1806, 1822 (2, above), 1823 (above), 1829, 1830 (above), 1837, 1838, 1853, 1854 (3), 1856, 1858, 1862, 1875, 1880, 1882, 1889, 1896 and 1904.

The wreck of the brig *Anna* in 1810 with the loss of ten lives inspired the

Cromer Lifeboat Committee to found the lifeboat station in Mundesley, and public subscriptions paid for the first purpose-built lifeboat in 1811. From 1823 to 1845 Lieutenant (Retired) Robert Rust was paid £3 a year to care for the boat. The Norfolk Association for Saving the Lives of Shipwrecked Mariners ran the lifeboat station until 1857 - along with those of Cromer, Bacton, and Winterton. The Royal National Lifeboat Institution took over in 1857 and introduced Mundesley's first self-righting 'Beak Class' boat in 1858. The boat, propelled by ten oars, cost £186.9s.5d and its launching carriage £37. It famously saved eleven lives from the wreck of the barque *Elizabeth & Mary* of Whitby in 1866. In the same year a bigger and better boat was commissioned: the *Grocers* cost £290.2s.3d and its launching carriage £78.2s. Thomas Gaze built its boathouse for £141 to the east of the Dell slope to the beach: it survives as a much altered private house. On 17 November 1868 the *Grocers* went to the aid of the brig *George* and William Juniper was awarded the RNLI Silver Medal for his bravery in rescuing the only sailor to survive the wreck. Another lifeboat *The J H Elliott* was presented by Mrs Elliott in memory of her husband in 1882. The RNLI boats saved fifty-one lives in fifteen launchings between 1858 and 1895, when the RNLI withdrew from Mundesley. Since 1972 the Mundesley Volunteer Inshore Lifeboat has provided cover to a high standard in inshore waters.

The Watch House and Signal Station on the cliff at Mundesley was built in 1812 for the Preventive Service (founded in 1809) together with the

Admiralty Cottages for its officers. The Preventive Service was renamed the Coastguard in 1822. In 1851 the chief officer of the coastguard was John Douglas; his men were George Evans, John Jones, Richard Lindup, Griffith Roberts, Thomas Toms and John Wright, three of whom served as boatmen. John Douglas and five of his men inhabited the Admiralty or now the Coastguard Cottages, which hide away at the end of Victoria Road, but John Wright lived in lodgings. Two retired coastguards were named as Richard Abbs and John Meacham. From the start the Watch House stored the Manby mortar. Invented soon after 1806 by Captain George William Manby and first used in a successful rescue in 1808, this substantial piece of life-saving equipment fired a cord into the rigging of a distressed vessel so that the crew could be hauled ashore in a *'breeches buoy.'* From 1814 rocket stations established round the coast saved many lives. Some other life-saving apparatus, notably an auxiliary hand-held rocket-launcher and an emergency lamp for beach and cliff rescues, is displayed in the Museum, but sadly not the mortar. Mundesley's Rocket Station was still operating in 1912. In 1883 the Chief Officer of the Coastguard was John Scammell, in 1912 Frederick William Richardson: each had a staff of four men. The present Watch Tower was erected in 1928 to replace the one built in 1812. Although the Coastguard has been withdrawn, the volunteers of the National Coastwatch have manned the Watch Tower since 1994.

Wrecks often led to sales of ships' wreckage and salvaged cargoes at the

Lifeboat Inn, Wheatley's Yard or in a field near the Watch House: rigging, spars, planking, and items such as 'spoiled wheat' or railway sleepers. The Museum displays a few salvaged items, notably a wine bottle from the Walkure wrecked on Haisborough Sands in December 1911. The ship's wheel and other items from the MV Jonet, wrecked in March 1969, are also in the Museum's collection. The name of the vessel survives in the Jonet Restaurant on Beach Road.

Smuggling

Before the era of free trade became firmly established in the second quarter of the nineteenth century, the high excise duties on tea, tobacco and spirits made smuggling profitable. In 1757 Henry Webster was committed to Norwich Castle for smuggling near Mundesley. An officer of the Preventive Service was stationed at Mundesley and in 1771 *'Mr Chris Cutting, riding officer at Mundesley, seized with the assistance of two dragoons, ... 946 lbs of tea, 5 casks of geneva [gin], and 12 papers of tobacco at Bacton beach.'* In 1822 the Preventive Service at Mundesley seized tobacco, brandy and geneva from a vault in a field at Witton. Similar discoveries were made in 1824 and 1826, and in 1829 Captain De Lafosse, the officer at Mundesley, traced what he thought was contraband to the Antingham house of the brothers Ireland, who refused him entry. While he went to find the magistrate, a cart was driven away. No goods were found and the brothers were able to appeal their conviction. The Museum displays some revenue officer's manacles or handcuffs.

A self-sufficient village?

Nineteenth century directories name craftsmen and traders, and many of the censuses list the occupations of those they counted. For example from the census of 1851 we can establish what employments were followed by people in the parish. We have already noted above the eight farmers and their labourers; the millers and their men; the fishermen, the sailors, and the coastguards. To this list the census of 1851 adds the practitioners of many crafts and trades:

Blacksmiths	James Coe, George Pyecraft, Robert Watson, Thomas Watson.
Bricklayers	William M Gotts, Martin Smith (labourer).
Builder	William Gaze, who employed three men.
Carpenters	William Watson, Josiah Winch.
Carriers	Richard Everard, Robert Grey, George Gray (& postman).
Carters	Robert Fuller, James Mack (coal carter).
Coal merchants	Robert Lacey, Thomas Woodhouse.

Cooper	Benjamin Hastings.
Dressmakers and needlewomen	Maria Breeze, Sarah Burton, Mary Ann Clarke, Elizabeth Claxton, Elizabeth Cooke, Jemima Kirby, Susanna Shingles, Mary Ann Turner, Elizabeth Wegg. Sarah Claxton appears as a tailor's wife, probably in her husband's temporary absence.
Gardeners	Valentine Barber, Thomas Cooke, Samuel Fuller, William Woodhouse.
Grocers	Robert Smith, Christopher Youngman.
Painters	Job Turner Winch, John Hastings (& glazier).
Postman	William Pratt, described as a 'letter-carrier.'
Ratcatcher	Joseph Loads (also described as a pauper).
Rabbit-seller	Sarah Loads.
Shoemakers	Thomas Farrow, John Wegg, Mark Wegg.
Tailors	Abraham Leman, William Spooner (each employing 1 man).
Washerwomen	Louisa Clarke, Mary Rudram, Mary, Anna & Ellen Withers.

The people on this list mostly worked with their hands. There were only two shopkeepers, but it was then common for farmers to sell produce from their farms or at market. The nearest market to Mundesley was at North Walsham. After farm labourers, servants were the largest group of workers, thirty-seven in all: of these all but nine were aged 13 to 25, and only two were male. Of the older nine four were general servants, four housekeepers and one a cook. Eleven people were described as paupers, but the seven under retirement age all had jobs, suggesting that their ability to work was limited by sickness or handicap.

'White collar' workers were few in number. To the school teachers noted above, we can add only eight:

Accountant	Thomas Hastings.
Clergy	The Rector Robert Steele, William Gordon (a non-officiating Anglican), Joseph Lawson Siddons (Rector of Edingthorpe).
Fund holder (? stockbroker)	Edward Henry Cormick.
Land agent	William Barcham.
Parish Clerk (employed by the church)	Samuel Cockman.
Proprietor of houses	Emma Fletcher

The census does not mention doctors or nurses, but in 1905 the church magazine praised the newly-formed federation of Mundesley, Knapton, Paston, Bacton, Witton and Edingthorpe to provide two district nurses. Their services were 'free' for an annual subscription that started at 2s for labourers or could be paid for as needed: there was no welfare state. At that date Dr Alex Wortley Quait seems to have been Mundesley's first resident doctor, living in the late Victorian St Brannock's in Cromer Road: he was the physician, surgeon and medical officer for the Mundesley district of the Erpingham Poor Law Union. Dr John Shepheard, medical officer for the Southrepps District, had a surgery in the nineteenth century Ocean View (now the Haig Club).

Figure 27: The initials of George Gordon on the facade of Gordon House

More shops appeared as Mundesley developed into an Edwardian seaside resort. The commercial centre of the village grew around the junction of Station Road and High Street. Some new premises were erected and older ones were adapted.

George Gordon built Gordon House, 32-36 High Street, in 1898: it still bears his initials. At its southern end George

Spurgeon ran Mundesley's first purpose-built butcher's shop, though Joseph Clarke was already plying his trade as a butcher in 1883 and George E Frostick from 1897: both were still operating in 1912. The butchery in Gordon House later moved round the corner into thatched premises in Station Road. From 1906 Walter Mace sold boots and shoes in the southern end of Gordon House, though his manager Arthur Robert Steward soon took over the business. The northern shop was that of the chemist William Dennis, who was soon succeeded by E Gane Inge *'Pharmacist & Optician, dealer in photographic apparatus and material.'* By 1912 Mr Inge had moved across the road to premises in Osborne House once occupied by Herbert J Whincup (see below), and A R Steward then moved his shoe shop next door and expanded into clothing.

The Post Office moved around Victorian and Edwardian Mundesley. In 1877 Miss Eliza Cooke was the sub-postmistress in East Hill House: letters arrived there from North Walsham at 8.20 am and were despatched at 2.45 pm. Adonijah Haggith, a tailor and shopkeeper in Back Street, became the sub-postmaster in 1880, but soon passed the business on to his son Jabez, a grocer in High Street. Jabez moved his business into Osborne House, 17-19 High Street, which was built in 1896 on the site of one of Ivy Farm's barns: sadly the shop building no longer bears its name. Later Jabez Haggith transferred his business to his son-in-law, Herbert J Whincup. The Post Office then moved at an uncertain date to 6 Cromer Road: the new sub-postmaster was Herbert D Bullard, who also sold stationery and china. In 1910 the Post Office moved again to its present location, when J Hartnall Limmer, who had operated as a house

Figure 29: The fading evidence of Norton T Wakelin's Circulating Library

(or estate) agent in a building that had been erected by T L Wakelin around 1900, became the sub-postmaster. Quite soon Norton T Wakelin took over as sub-postmaster, a position he held for over forty years. He also owned and ran the Mundesley Circulating Library in 1912. Over many years he made a huge contribution to the religious and sporting life of Mundesley.

Melbourne House, the shop on the corner of High Street and Cromer Road appears to date from the turn of the twentieth century, as does the shop opposite at 4 Cromer Road. In 1912 Melbourne House was occupied by Newton & Larter, grocers, drapers and milliners, who also offered apartments in the summer season.

No seaside resort could be without its photographer: William Allard plied his trade from one of the Royal Cottages (behind the Royal Hotel in Beckmeadow Way): his was the cottage nearest to the Beck.

To these Edwardian traders *Kelly's Directory* of 1912 adds quite a number more, usually without mentioning the location of their premises: Barclays Bank, which opened on Tuesdays and Fridays in July, August and September, but only on Fridays in other months (at 6 Cromer Road?); Ernest Burnett, baker; Robert Clarke, fishmonger; Benjamin Cooper, fruiterer; George Thomas Gaze, baker in Marlborough House; Herbert William Hayden, tobacconist; William Holt, ironmonger; Emma Lester, dairy; Arthur Hammond Minns, bookseller; Anna Neale, fancy repository (gift shop?); Elizabeth Perkins, draper; Arthur George Perry, boot-maker; Stanley Simmons & Co, house agents; George Twigg, watchmaker; and Webster & Bell, grocers in Graham House.

7. MUNDESLEY AS A SEASIDE RESORT

A health cure by the sea?

The benefits of breathing sea air and bathing in sea-water were advocated from the eighteenth century. In 1770 Richard Moneys of Mundesley advertised a bathing machine to enable swimmers to change discreetly before being wheeled into the sea. In 1791 a local shopkeeper, John Kidd, offered both lodgings with a sea view and a new bathing machine with careful attendants. In 1795 and 1796 the poet and hymn-writer William Cowper (1731-1800) holidayed in Mundesley in the hope that the sea air would cure his melancholia (depressive illness): he gave his name to Cowper House in the High Street. These were small beginnings, and in 1806 Edward Bartel called Mundesley *'a straggling village, little worthy of notice'* and continued: *'There is one bathing machine, and some few, though the number is small, frequent Mundesley in the bathing season. The accommodations are very confined. Four or five houses at the most appear all calculated for the purposes of lodgings, and these are situated close to the side of a dusty road.'*

The discovery of a mineral spring in Mundesley led to a proposal in 1823 for a spa offering the same healing properties as Harrogate and Aix-la-

Chapelle, but it came to nothing. Even so by 1836 *White's Directory of Norfolk* rates Mundesley as a bathing place next to Cromer, and speaks of neat modern houses offering apartments during the bathing season, of two good inns and several lodging houses with bathing machines, and of John Larter's warm bath-house. *White's* goes on: *'Mundesley has been much improved during the last ten or twelve years by the spirited exertions of F Wheatley, Esq (Vice Admiral of the Coast), who has built a handsome mansion on the cliff; and to preserve it from the encroachments of the sea has lately erected at the cost of £1000, two massive walls, forming an upper and lower terrace, the latter of which, being 90 feet above the beach, commands an extensive marine prospect.'*

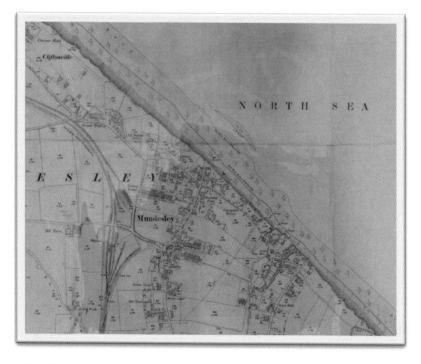

Figure 30: The 1905 Ordnance Survey map showing the railway (by courtesy of Ordnance Survey)

MUNDESLEY AS A SEASIDE RESORT

The railway comes to Mundesley

In 1885 a magazine article showed how isolated Mundesley still was from the outside world: *'The telegraph wires have not yet reached Mundesley, the posts are not too frequent and the daily papers can only be obtained with difficulty.'* However Mr R W Palmer of the Black Swan Inn in North Walsham ran a daily horse omnibus to Mundesley in the summer season. In 1854 and 1883 there was a carrier to North Walsham daily and to Norwich twice a week. When in 1890 the family of Norton T Wakelin came to holiday in Mundesley, they came by the Great Eastern Railway to North Walsham and *'were met by the Mundesley village postman and general news vendor, who kept a pony and trap for fetching and carrying...'* The sea-front was undeveloped apart from the industrial and commercial centre around the Dell - that is, until the railway came.

The railway (NHER 13585) reached Mundesley from North Walsham in 1898 and from Cromer in 1906, a joint venture of the Midland and Great Northern Joint Railway (M&GN) and the Great Eastern Railway (GER). The line was constructed by Mr Mousley of Rugby. The impressive station, built by Cornish & Gaymer of North Walsham, anticipated the extension of the line to Cromer: it had three 600 foot platforms, one bay and a passing loop. The whole project was supervised by Mr W Marriott of the M&GN. The railway was operated alternately year by year by the

GER and the M&GN. Steam expresses arrived from London via Norwich and North Walsham and somewhat slower trains from the Midlands via Melton Constable and Cromer.

The line to North Walsham opened on 20 June 1898. It passed through the intermediate station of Paston & Knapton and in North Walsham had access to both the GER Main Station and the M&GN Town Station. The first passenger train from Mundesley at 7.35 am on 8 July carried a hundred children from the Board School and took on a further sixty at Knapton. Steam engines drew the sixteen, later fourteen, trains a day until 1956 when diesel multiple units were introduced. At a lunch held at the Clarence Hotel on 1 July 1898 to celebrate the opening of the railway, the Chairman said he *'believed that there was no place more beneficial for the man whose brain is overwrought in which to recuperate than Mundesley-on-Sea.'* The railway played a major role in developing Mundesley as a seaside resort in the early twentieth century and in bringing many more people to make their home in the village. In 1912 the station master was Thomas H Murrell.

The line to Cromer shut on 6 April 1953 and the Beeching Plan of 1963 led to the closure of the line to North Walsham to passenger traffic on 4 October 1964 and to freight on 28 December, even though it was still making a profit of £3,000 a year. The single track was lifted in 1966-67, and the station and the three bridges in the village were demolished. The site of the station is now occupied by modern housing, but you can still see Railway Terrace built for the railway's staff and the artificial rise in Station Road created to carry the roadway over the railway bridge. Much of the line in both directions can still be traced through the landscape. An unusual survival in the front garden of a dwelling in Trunch Road is a railway carriage (NHER 18469): it may have been built for the GER or M&GN in the late nineteenth century. The car and the bus now rule, but the Eastern Counties bus station in Cromer Road, active after World War II, is no more. When did the Mundesley Garage Company set up business beside the Manor Hotel and when did it move to the High Street?

Figure 31: The sign at Mundesley on Sea railway station

Poppyland and Cliftonville

On 30 August 1883 the poet and theatre critic Clement Scott (1841-1904) began a series of articles in the *Daily Telegraph* extolling the rural idyll on the coast between Sheringham and Mundesley. He christened

Figure 32: The name plate of St Cecilia's villa

this area 'Poppyland' and penned a famous poem - *The Garden of Sleep* - as he waited beside the ruins of Sidestrand's church tower for Louie Jermy, the miller's daughter with whom he had fallen in love. Encouraged by the public response to Poppyland and the prospect of rail links from London to Mundesley, developers proposed to create the Cliftonville Estate on the West Cliff with shops, hotels, a promenade and a pier. A first sale of land on and near Cromer Road in 1889 saw every plot sold. However when 153 plots on Seaview Road were offered for sale on 6 April 1890, many remained unsold, because a large cliff fall a few days before posed serious questions about their long-term viability. However some properties were built along Sea View Road, notably the Clarence Hotel and the large villa of St Cecilia's with its fine ceramic name plate giving the date of 1890. St Olaf's, 116 Cromer Road, has a name stone that includes the name of Cliftonville.

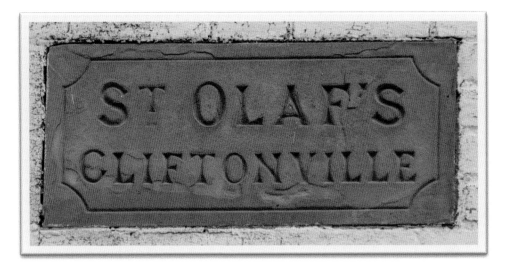

Figure 33: The only (?) physical evidence of the name of Cliftonville

Building the seaside: stabilising the cliffs and the beach

Erosion not only threatened the cliffs but also the stability of the beach. The walls built to defend Cliff House by Mr Wheatley were hardly finished when they were badly damaged in severe storms in 1836 and 1845 and required substantial repairs. In 1862 another great storm caused serious cliff falls with the loss of some seven yards of land across much of the sea-front and the destruction of the accesses to the beach: the lifeboat ramp alone survived but in a damaged state. In 1897 waves driven by fierce gales did huge damage: much of Town End was lost and with it a section of the road which until the nineteenth century had passed in front of Church Cottages and behind the School to Town End.

The gangways to the beach were again destroyed. As a result Steward & Patteson, the owners of the Ship Inn, built a sea wall and breakwater to protect the cliff beneath their property; they also made an opening through the cliff to allow public access to the beach. Further action followed: in 1908 a public promenade was built westwards from Steward & Patteson's sea wall to the Manor Hotel's private promenade, from which it was separated by a small gap. Along the new promenade a concrete wall eighteen inches high was constructed to protect the bottom of the cliff and two gangways descending from close to the Watch House made access much easier. Only four years later the great storm of 1912 seriously damaged the promenade. In the 1940s Sandho Lodge, a small private hotel on the cliff edge, was demolished because of erosion. By 1950 the Rev John Gedge, Rector of All Saints since 1946, became so concerned at the cliff erosion threatening the Church that he petitioned the Crown, the patron of the benefice, to expedite the further defence of the cliff bottom: the defences were extended to the west using obsolete tramlines and concrete blocks. However storm and tide have continued to cause severe problems, notably in the storm surges of 1953 and 2013.

Making the beach safe and attractive

A rather sad memorial tablet in All Saints' Church reminds us that the unpredictable sea and its currents require bathers to exercise caution: *'Sacred to the memory of Robert Delpratt Esquire, a youth of the most amiable disposition and the most promising acquirements whose remains are interred in the aisle of this church. His afflicted relatives and friends were suddenly deprived of him on the 18th of Sept. 1819 in the 18th year of his age (while bathing) by an unforeseen and rapid current on the*

Figure 34: The memorial to Robert Delpratt

neighbouring Coast. This small but heartfelt tribute of affection for him is humbly offered by his disconsolate parents.' He was not the first, nor the last: William Rees, Master of the Paston School and Curate of Mundesley, died of *'apoplexy whilst bathing at Mundesley'* in 1835 and a visitor from London drowned while swimming in 1898. The cliffs have never been safe to climb: a man was killed in a cliff fall in 1930.

Today bathers in the sea or sun are protected by the RNLI Lifeguards, the Inshore Lifeboat and the National Coastwatch Institution. From 1902 these were preceded by the bathing protection boat *Richard C Garlick*. The boat, housed and launched by George Johnson & Son until 1912, was on duty for one and a half hours before breakfast and for four hours afterwards - but not after breakfast on Sundays! The boat saved two ladies and a man in 1906.

The beach was central to the enjoyment of Edwardian visitors. By 1910 the Parish Council had control of it and set the charges: bathing machines cost 5s for the season; cabins and tents 6d per week; and chairs 9d per dozen per week. It seems that these facilities were operated by George Johnson & Son until 1912 when a storm destroyed their equipment and drove them out of business, to Parish Council's regret. Concessions were offered for a fee: Mr Bennett sold tea coffee and milk from 6.00 am to 10.00 am for a fee of 2s a week; Mrs Harmer paid a fee of 2s 6d to sell refreshments on August Bank Holiday; while hirers of donkeys paid 6d per beast per day, and it cost 1s a day to hawk (peddle) one's goods. The grocers Messrs Webster & Bell formed the Beach Catering Company in 1913 but it only lasted until the outbreak of war in 1914.

Figure 35: The Watch Tower of 1928 which houses the Museum stands on the clifftop. Close by is the memorial to those who were gave their lives clearing mines in 1944-53 and in the distance is the Manor Hotel

The greens beside the Watch Tower at the top of the gangways down to the beach have pavilions that date from the 1930s.

Other attractions for visitors and residents

Many activities became available to villagers and visitors in Edwardian Mundesley. Those inclined towards sport found cricket and football clubs active on the Recreation Ground, which, owned by Henry Fielder Johnson, stretched from Mundesley House to Marina Road. Held there were the annual Charity Football Shield on Good Friday (Mundesley won it for the first time in 1907) and the Athletic Sports Meeting on the second Saturday in August. The

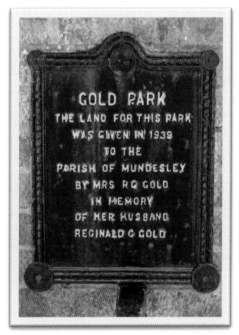

Figure 36: The dedication at the entrance to Gold Park

Recreation Ground was given to the people of Mundesley in 1939 by Mrs Anna Randall and Mrs Ruby Gold and was renamed Gold Park in memory of Mrs Gold's husband Reginald.

Sir Samuel Hoare, the first president of Mundesley Golf Club, struck the first ball on the nine hole course on 20 July 1901, and Mundesley's

87

professional Richard Kelly won the exhibition match against Caistor's professional James Bailey by one hole. The original subscription was a guinea, but half a guinea for women when the Ladies' Section was formed in 1903, and visitors paid 2s a day in the summer and 1s in winter. In 1924 further land was purchased and an eighteen hole course was opened on 4 August. In World War II part of the course was ploughed up to grow food. The eighteen holes seem to have been reinstated after the war, but the course reverted to nine holes in 1948. A new clubhouse was built in 1976.

The old reading room was condemned as insanitary and its replacement, the Mundesley Institute, was founded in a house called High Cliff, built in 1891 and bought in 1908 for £1250. It was vested in a board of trustees in 1911, of which Mr E A Lucas was the secretary. At one point it was called the Toc H Building, after the wartime refuge for soldiers founded by the Rev Tubby Clayton in Flanders. The house offered rooms for reading, billiards, other games, society meetings and education, and provided accommodation for the resident caretaker. The grounds of two acres provided a bowling green, tennis courts and garden plots. For 2d a week (1d for youths) or 2s a quarter members could enjoy many activities. When the Institute closed in the 1970s, the land was purchased by Mrs Gedge, wife of the late Rector, for use by All Saints: it is now the church car park. Next door the Coronation Hall was opened by Sir Samuel Hoare on 6 August 1912, when Mr E A Lucas was the secretary.

When the village celebrated King George V's coronation in 1910, £77.1s.4d was left over, which became the seed corn for the raising of nearly £700 to fund the Hall. It built by the firm of S A Randall to the designs of George Michael Silley, a London architect who grew fond of Mundesley and made it his home. The Hall proved a popular venue for meetings and entertainments.

Flies, horse-drawn carriages, could in 1912 be hired for excursions from Larter Brothers or from Frederick Keymer.

A photograph taken in 1897 when the Methodist Chapel was being built shows a performing bear: how times have changed!

Accommodating the visitors

The visitors attracted to Mundesley's sea and sand needed places to stay. The census of 1851 lists four lodging house keepers: Elizabeth Andrews, Mary Ann Cooke, Phoebe Cox and Rebecca Russell. In 1883 lodging houses were run by Sarah Ann Cook, Robert Dix, and Daniel Pull. They no doubt housed villagers as well as visitors. By 1912 there were six lodging houses, then called boarding houses, and thirty private dwellings offered apartments in the summer season, many of them in Mundesley's late Victorian and Edwardian housing such as Katherine Villas in Manor Road, Russell Terrace and Victoria Cottages. Some regular visitors bought or built houses: the Institute was a converted holiday home.

The more wealthy could stay in one of Mundesley's hotels. Three were of long standing:

- The Royal Hotel was until 1879 the New Inn, where reputedly Horatio Nelson, educated at the Paston School in 1769-71, stayed during school holidays. Charles Boughey was its landlord in 1851, George Young Smith in 1883 and Edward James Gray in 1912. It was owned by the Norwich Brewers Steward & Patteson from 1877. A third storey was added in the early 1900s.

- The (Old) Ship Hotel or Inn may have originated in 1802 and was owned by the Juniper family: Robert Juniper was its innkeeper in 1851, William S Juniper in 1883. From the late nineteenth century it was owned by Steward & Patteson and had a bowls green and a quoit bed. *Kelly's Directory of Norfolk* lists Robert William Cross as its proprietor (landlord?) in 1912.

- The Lifeboat Inn, 23 Beach Road, is said to have been the oldest pub in the village. The landlord was Thomas Woodhouse in 1854, Emma Fox in 1883, Frederick Wilson in 1912. In 1912 it was owned by Steward & Patteson and from 1967 by Watney Mann, who closed it in c.1984.

These three hotels were joined by at least six more:

- The Clarence Hotel, built as part of Cliftonville in 1891, ceased trading in 1938. It then became a convalescent home, which was owned by the London Borough of Haringey from 1941 to 1987.

Figure 37: Trafalgar Court, once the Grand Hotel

- The Grand Hotel was built on a site purchased in 1890 to the sumptuous designs of Herbert J Green, sometime architect for the Diocese of Norwich (see the frontispiece on page ii). The entrance hall and stairs survive in all their grandeur. Church services were held there during the rebuilding of All Saints in 1903 by permission of the manager, Mr Vogel. Reilly Mead is listed as the proprietor in 1912. Commandeered by the forces during World War II, the Grand later reappeared as the Hotel Continental. After closure in c.1990, it was converted to apartments and renamed

Trafalgar Court.

Figure 38: Looking up the fine stairwell of the Grand Hotel to the dome in the roof

- The Manor House Hotel was commissioned by Bullards Brewery, designed by J B Pearce and built in 1898 in an ornate style worthy of a national listing. Miss I A Beesley was its proprietor (landlady?) in 1912. The Manor's private promenade at the bottom of the cliff was accessed by a white-painted wooden staircase.

Figure 39: The Bullards Brewery insignia on the west wall of the Manor Hotel

- The Abbeville Hotel, formerly Cliff Brow, was built by George Gray of Paston as part of the Cliftonville Estate in c1890. It stood west of the Clarence Hotel and adopted its new name in 1900. Cliff erosion led to its demolition in the 1950s.

- The Seaview House Hotel, which was once operative in Paston Road, is now apartments. In 1912 Mary Ann Dix offered apartments there in the summer season.

- Cliff House, which stands on the cliff above the Dell, was a hotel between 1945 and 1972.

The Mundesley Holiday Centre on the East Cliff, just beyond the parish boundary, opened in 1933, the first in Norfolk and second in England only to Brighthouse on the Isle of White, which opened in 1930. Both were the idea of Victor Edwards. The octagonal layout of the buildings reflected the pattern of the sails of Stow Mill, opposite the Centre's driveway off Paston Road. The central building housed both the pump that drew water from an artesian well and the generator that provided all the electricity. There were 172 chalets, sleeping one to four people and giving a total capacity of 360. All had cold water, but hot had to be collected from central taps. The Centre was self-contained and offered a complete social life with good facilities such as a ballroom, tennis courts, putting green, croquet, bowls and football. The swimming pool came in 1967. Wooden steps gave access to the beach but fell victim to cliff erosion, making a descent perilous by the 1980s. Beach access may have been less vital by then because from the 1970s the Centre upgraded its chalets and concentrated on holidays for the over-50s. Other chalet and caravan parks have opened, mainly on the outskirts of the settlement area.

In the village Paston Road was home to Raxawa, a Youth House or Holiday Home of the Methodist Church of Great Britain. Raxawa is now the Tamil name for a tea estate in central Sri Lanka which was, it seems, connected with the Wesleyan Methodist Mission to Ceylon, established in 1814. In Mundesley Raxawa offered good residential facilities with indoor and outdoor activities to youth groups from just after World War II until the 1990s: the records of the Raxawa Trust cover 1947-93. Its former large site is now occupied by modern housing.

Taking the cure in the sea air: the Sanatorium

The wealthy who could afford the high fee of five guineas a week came to benefit from the sea air at the private sanatorium built in 1899 by Dr Burton-Fanning, who later wrote *The Open Air Treatment of Tuberculosis* (1905). The sectional timber building, designed and built by Boulton & Paul of Norwich, was delivered by sea and erected in extensive grounds. The Sanatorium had its own vegetable gardens and poultry farm, obtained its milk from the tested herd of a nearby farm, drew its water from a well dug down into the chalk and filtered it to make it soft. The sanatorium's treatment of tuberculosis was based on the open-air methods pioneered by Swiss and German doctors. Patients were housed in chalets that could be rotated to face the sun and avoid the wind: despite the sheltered site south-west of the village, patients must have found it cold in winter! Each patient was given a carefully calculated diet and followed a programme of graduated exercise. By 1902 the Sanatorium had treated 143 patients, and claimed that 121 had had their disease halted or improved. Dr Sidney Vere Pearson, who had suffered from tuberculosis himself, was appointed as the medical superintendent in 1905 and later became a part-owner. The Sanatorium was the first of its kind in Britain and its original building is listed II by English Heritage. A large extension was built in 1923. When medication was found that could control tuberculosis, the National Health Service adopted the Sanatorium in 1957 and turned it into a rehabilitation unit in 1960 under the name of Mundesley Hospital, even though it lies in the parish of Gimingham. After closure in 1992-93, it reopened in 1997 as the Diana Princess of Wales Treatment Centre for Drug and Alcohol

Problems. Financial problems forced it to close in 2008, but the Hope Community has reopened it.

Figure 40: The brick kiln on the West Cliff (by courtesy of the Kiln Cliffs Caravan Park)

8. THE BUILDINGS OF MUNDESLEY

The materials

There is little stone in Norfolk apart from flint, and in the Middle Ages only the builders of All Saints' Church could afford to bring limestone by sea from Caen in Normandy or from Barnack near Peterborough. Even in the church limestone was only used where carvings or corners required it, and the church walls were built of flint set in lime mortar. Elsewhere in the parish little has survived of earlier, impermanent building materials, such as timber-framing infilled with wattle and daub or with mud brick. However two carved wooden heads (NHER 39454), found in a secondary location in Medlar Place in the High Street in 2002, may have come from a late medieval ecclesiastical hammer-beam roof or from a late medieval or early post-medieval jetty of a house. Mundesley's earlier houses and gardens often have flint cobble walls. Many of the flints were picked off ploughed fields, but it was easier to take flint cobbles, gravel and shingle from the beach. However concern that such removals were adding to the erosion of the cliffs led to a ban in 1912.

Two companies provided most of the bricks used in Mundesley's building boom of 1890-1914: the Mundesley Brick and Tile Company on the West Cliff within the present Kiln Cliffs Caravan Park; and Williment Brothers on the East Cliff near the Mundesley Holiday Centre. The partnership between James and Robert Williment was dissolved on 24 June 1909, with Robert assuming responsibility for its debts: he was still operating as a builder in 1912. The kiln on the West Cliff (NHER 14141) is listed II because it is believed to be the only surviving 'haystack' kiln in Norfolk, where such kilns were common in the north-east of the county. Dating from the early nineteenth century, it is conical in shape and is bound with iron bands. A round-headed doorway opens into the kiln while a sunken entry gives access to the stoke hole. It was converted to a dwelling in the twentieth century with windows and a clock (which reputedly came from the station), but is no longer used as such. Nearby is the drying shed with a pantile roof. The pug mill was operated by a horse following a circular path. Both brickworks produced the soft red Norfolk brick characteristic of many Edwardian houses in Mundesley.

The utilities

When the railway arrived there was no piped water. So the engines were watered from the Beck, and the Larter Brothers, who ran the watermill and had jurisdiction over the Beck from Gimingham to Mundesley, were given £10 a year in compensation. Water taken from the Beck had long

Figure 41: The Water-works built in 1899

been thought unfit to drink: a sheep dip lay upstream! So drinking water was obtained from the water carrier William Bensley at a ha'penny a pail or from the village pump, of which a Victorian photograph exists. It was felt that, if Mundesley were to attract visitors piped water was essential. Erpingham Rural District Council established the water-works in 1899. A well was sunk opposite Beck Cottages on the High Street well away from the salt of the sea. Chalk was found ninety feet down and a well of cast iron cylinders was constructed to that depth. A further hundred feet was bored into the chalk and water rose up into the iron well. Water was then pumped via an iron pipe to a reservoir on the cliff west of Cliftonville, giving a head of water to supply the village. At first water

99

Figure 42: The only remaining standpipe by the Watch Tower

was provided at standpipes in the village (only the one by the Watch Tower survives), but by 1908 every house had a piped water supply. The village pond, used for watering draught animals, lay where the entrance to Gold Park now is. Probably the arrival of the standpipes led to its infilling in 1902. Sewers and drains were installed in the village in 1903.

Piped water encouraged the Parish Council to buy some limited fire-fighting equipment, but a public meeting in November 1900 resolved to raise funds to purchase a manual fire engine and form a Volunteer Fire Brigade. Jack Kitteringham, the water-works' manager, was the captain: he and his crew trained once a quarter, for which they were paid 1s.6d. The fire engine was kept in the Rectory's coach-house in Paston Road, until George Gray built the Fire Engine House in Back Street in 1907 on the site of the 'Doctor's Pit.' The restored Fire Engine House is the office of Mundesley Parish Council, established under the Local Government Act of 1894: its clerk in 1912 was Alfred Larter. The manual fire engine served until 1938, when a secondhand steam fire engine was obtained from Cromer. World War II exposed the lack of standardisation in the fitments used by local brigades and a National Fire Service was created in 1941, though it was itself replaced by county services in 1948. Norfolk County Council built the new Fire Station in Trunch Road in 1965 and it became operational in 1966.

Figure 43: The Fire Station in the 1940s restored as the office of the Parish Council

Town gas arrived in 1903 when the Mundesley gas-works opened under the auspices of the Mundesley and Holt Gas Company. At first there werc ten street lamps, lit by lamplighter Lewis 'Brantley' Broom at 4.30 pm and extinguished at 10.30 pm, but there were fifty-two by 1947. Gas-lighting and gas-cooking were quite widely adopted. The gas-works sold its by-products to offset its costs: coke was supplied to Sanatorium with the spare going to Thomas Moy's coalyard at the station; tar (nine gallons from each ton of coal) went to a refinery in Yarmouth. At the start the manager was Edmund Craske, with assistants Lewis Broom and

Percy Harris. The manager was John Hallows in 1912 and Bernard Clarke in 1956, when the works closed.

Electricity seems to have arrived in the early 1930s (All Saints' organ was powered by an electric pump from 1934), but before then a few nearby houses used electricity generated by Larter's Mill.

Figure 44: The 1884 OS map, showing Mundesley before its late Victorian and Edwardian expansion (by courtesy of Ordnance Survey)

Mundesley's housing

The church, chapels, hotels and shops have been discussed above, and so this section concentrates on Mundesley's houses. Many of the older dwellings stand in large plots framed by decorative flint and brick walls which add character to the village.

The late Victorian and Edwardian building boom is clearly shown by a comparison of the first and second editions of the Ordnance Survey maps of 1884 and 1905. Mr G M Silley, honorary architect for the Coronation Hall, formed the East Coast Estates Company to buy

Figure 45: The ornate west gable end of Russell Terrace

up land and property for the purpose of development as Mundesley grew into a seaside resort. Quite a number of houses in Mundesley are in the Art and Crafts style of Russell Terrace and of Millstream (now 27-37 Beckmeadow Way) built in 1904 and 1909 respectively by the firm of Sidney Arthur Randall. The firm also acted as the agent for Cliff Farm

Lands and Estate and for the East Coast Estates Company. Other late Victorian or Edwardian terraces include Victoria Cottages built for T L Wakelin at £99 each (Victoria Road); Wortley Terrace and Trafalgar Terrace on Cromer Road; Railway Terrace and Manor Road, both off Church Lane.

The High Street contains many notable dwellings:

- Mundesley House is no. 1 High Street (odd numbers on the east side) and stands in a large plot on the corner with Beach Road. An earlier and smaller flint house with brick dressings was remodelled in brick in the early nineteenth century. The new L-plan property has a fine two-storey southern facade in the late Georgian style.

- Manor Cottage, no. 8 (even numbers on the west side), was built of rendered brick in the mid to late nineteenth century. The name suggests the Manor House was next door: it stood on a large plot at the corner of High Street and Cromer Road before Melbourne House was built.

- Longford House, no. 16, is Victorian with a fine small pebble facade.

- Bay house, no. 18, was built in the grand style in Edwardian red brick.

- Next to the Post Office is the L-shaped Ivy Farmhouse: its east wing appears to date from the eighteenth century but the front of the higher north wing dates from the 1830s.

- The Old House, no. 28, lies behind Gordon House. The steep angle of its pantile roof indicates that it was once thatched. Its northern end has a Dutch gable perhaps of the late seventeenth or of the eighteenth century, but its chimney may be Victorian 'Tudor.'

Figure 46: The Dutch gable of the Old House

- The thatched Russell Cottage, no. 31, has a small pebble facade in late Georgian in style, perhaps of the 1830s.

- Cowper House, no. 33 (NHER 44614 - listed II), dates from the late eighteenth century, though Historic England lists it as later. This two-storey dwelling in rendered brick was once a farmhouse whose owner farmed 'The Fields' that stretched from the High Street to the Beck.

- Point House, where the High Street and Back Street diverge, belongs to the early nineteenth century.

- The Gables, no. 45, has crow-stepped gables which are decorated with diapering of brick set in flint, a later nineteenth century imitation of a sixteenth or early seventeenth century style.

- No. 49-51 and no. 53, on either side of the entrance to Beckmeadow Way, are two large Arts and Crafts dwellings reminiscent of many built by S A Randall in the early years of the twentieth century, especially the eastern facade of nos. 49-51.

- Prospect House, no. 60, is an early nineteenth century farmhouse.

- Northfield House, on the west side of the street, has been mentioned above in relation to the early twentieth century Bible conferences. Its early nineteenth century structure has been much altered.

- The long thatched, flint and brick barn (NHER 14140), now converted to a dwelling, lies north of the Grange on the east side of the street: it may have originated in the early eighteenth century because its date plaque seems to read 1714. The neighbouring barn is somewhat later.

- The Grange has a date stone of 1900 and is an elaborate Arts and Crafts house with brick diapering in its cobble walls and flint diapering in its three storey projecting porch.

Figure 47: The Grange, a fine example of the Arts and Crafts style

The front door is flanked by impressive decorative consoles. Its pantile roof has elaborate chimneys.

- Mundesley Beck House (NHER 14143 - listed II) was once the Rookery and the home of the major landowners Rev William Gordon in 1851 and the Rev Edward Gordon in 1914. It lies, largely hidden, east of the High Street but can also be accessed from Water Lane. Its two-storey facade of five bays was built in the early nineteenth century and its central projecting bay later in the century. Some of its flint rear and side walls may be earlier: a plaque in the west wall bears an early seventeenth century date.

- Moss Cottage, no. 80, is a gem. Its north gable has an early slit opening and brick-in-flint diapering that indicates a date in the later sixteenth or early seventeenth century. Its steep roof was once thatched but has been altered to raise the ceiling height of the rooms in the upper storey.

Figure 48: The gable end of Moss Cottage

- At the start of Water Lane is Fourways, a dwelling that began as two quite early cottages. They have been altered and extended, but vestiges of an early platband, perhaps of the late seventeenth or eighteenth century, survives between the storeys, and two former doors in the front have become windows.

Mundesley abounds in good late Victorian and Edwardian villas. The coast road features several: Baltimore (no. 5) and St Brannock's (no. 7) on Cromer Road; Barmston (no. 9) and Beach House (no. 10) on Beach Road; and Tower House (just past Bowman's Corner) in Paston Road.

There are also many fine brick and flint cottages. Good examples are the early nineteenth century Church Cottages near the former school in Cromer Road and the roadside cottages at the bottom of the Dell.

Two houses on the coast road are worthy of note:

- Cliff House, no. 1 Paston Road (just before Bowman's Corner), faces west and from its high position commands wide views over Mundesley and the sea. Built by Francis Wheatley in 1830, it is protected from cliff erosion by high sea walls. Below to the west lay the buildings and yards of Mr Wheatley's shipping, coal and timber businesses, now replaced by more modern housing.

Figure 49: Francis Wheatley's Cliff House overlooking his coal and timber yards in the Dell

- Dell Cottage, no. 14 Beach Road (NHER 44613 - listed II), lies in the bottom of the Dell and began life as two single-storey cottages. They were built in flint with brick dressings in the gothic style of the mid nineteenth century - not earlier as they do not appear on the Tithe Map. A modern conservatory obscures the façade but the Victorian 'Tudor' chimney is decorative.

Mundesley's Conservation Area

The Conservation Area was designated in 1975 and then had two parts: first, the buildings on either side of the full length of the High Street as far as Town End, with Russell Terrace, Victoria Road and Gold Park;

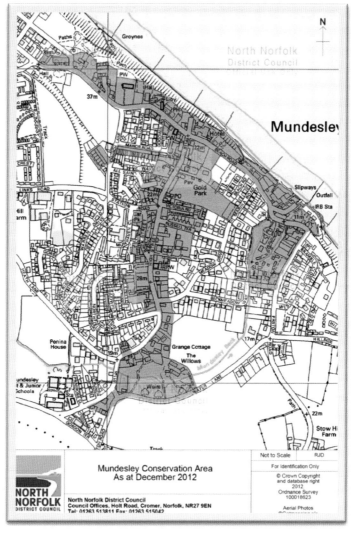

Figure 50: The map showing the Conservation Area (by courtesy of North Norfolk District Council)

111

and second, the land and buildings from the Ship Inn to the Royal including the Dell, the Mill Pond and the Royal Cottages. North Norfolk District Council consulted on the conservation area in June and early July 2009. Its *Character Appraisal and Management Proposals* proposed extending the Conservation Area in four ways: linking the two designated areas by including Beach Road and the greens by the Watch Tower; adding the public garden beside Gold Park; extending up Cromer Road up to Trafalgar Court; and widening the High Street corridor to include Manor Road and Railway Terrace. The *Character Appraisal* was adopted in November 2009 and a new map showing the extended conservation area was published in December 2012.

Conservation areas may have a lower profile now that reduced resources have drastically changed the priorities of local and national government. In the Local Development Framework of North Norfolk District Council Mundesley is a service village where further residential development is possible. We - and especially our local representatives - must be vigilant to defend the historic character of our built environment.

9. MUNDESLEY AT WAR

Mundesley at war before the twentieth century

There is little to connect Mundesley to warfare before 1914. However in the Hundred Years' War signal beacons were sited on the Norfolk coast from 1427, and in 1450 Margaret Paston writes about French raiders who kidnapped people from the shore to ransom them. A little later Agnes Paston says that French raiders seized two pilgrims but released them once their religious intent became known, and adds that the French took four ships from Cromer and Happisburgh. Some of the Paston family, who then owned property in Mundesley, were involved in the Wars of the Roses in the later fifteenth century and may have taken Norfolk retainers with them on campaign. NHER 15350 reports that a medieval or post-medieval culverin or small cannon was found on the beach at very low tide in 1979. It was not recovered but was about 75 cm in length with a bore of about 100 mm. If it was a culverin it is probable that it was no earlier in date than the sixteenth century. Was it perhaps part of England's defence against the Spanish Armada in 1588? The culverin would have played no role in the English Civil War of 1642-48, because there was no fighting in north-east Norfolk. Culverins were obsolete at least a century before 1803, when the fear of a French invasion caused fortifications to be built along the Norfolk coast, including a gun fort at Mundesley. No trace of the fort survives.

Mundesley in World War I

The outbreak of war saw the severance for security reasons of the new Anglo-German telegraph cable laid in 1913. It had made its landfall near the Ship Hotel.

Figure 51: The war memorial in All Saints' Church

Twenty-seven names appear on the First World War memorial in All

Saints' Church: Harrison Allen, Bernard Clarke, Walter G Earl, Thomas A J Everitt, James D H Farmer, Bertie G Gotts, Donald C Hair, Edward F Johnson, Ernest R Jordan, Douglas Lambert, L (Louis) G Lancaster, George W Lee, E Bernard Livermore, R Michael Mack, F Reg Mason, A (Alfred) J Matthews, Alfred Norton, Edward B Pedder, John Platten, John Puncher, F Victor Rudram, Austin G Rudram, Chas J Rudram, Edwin C Watson, Harry Watson, Oscar Welberry, and Harry Youngman. There are separate wall tablets to James Douglas Henry Farmer, to Thomas Henry Fielder Johnson, who died of his wounds in 1919, and Edward Fielder Johnson. Thomas Henry Fielder Johnson seems to have died too late to appear on the war memorial.

Mundesley played its part in coastal defence, though NHER carries no entries for defensive structures. However a mobile battery of six heavy field guns was stationed in the parish and a pillbox was built. And one of Britain's two armoured trains ran on the M&GN/GER line to Mundesley: it had four armoured wagons, two six-pounder guns and two machine guns. The first Zeppelin raid on England on 19 January 1915 made its landfall at Bacton: Zeppelin L3 turned south-east towards Yarmouth; Zeppelin L4 turned north-west, flying over Mundesley towards Sheringham and Hunstanton.

Mundesley in World War II

Fourteen names appear on the World War II memorial in All Saints' Church: Raymond Chase, Edward Clarke, Francis Davis, Reginald Gotts, Stanley Gotts, Malcolm Gunn, Robert Livermore, Edgar Myhill, Hugh Perry, John Rudram, Jack Shannahan, Edward Smith, John Thirst, and Hugh Wood.

It was thought likely that a German invasion force would choose north-east Norfolk as its landfall and a network of defensive structures was built along the coast. Most of Mundesley's cliff-top defences have fallen victim to coastal erosion. Two type 24 polygonal pill-boxes survive, both visible on aerial photos from 1941: one (NHER 18471) in the garden of

Figure 52: The pillbox behind 19 Marina Road

20 Beckmeadow Way overlooks the Beck and Water Lane; the other (NHER 18476) behind 19 Marina Road was probably connected to the seafront defences; there is some confusion over a third type 24 pillbox (NHER 14139). Tank traps and road blocks were deployed along the seafront and across roads, again seemingly in 1941: one (NHER 32620), made from concrete-filled oil drums, was reported on the beach in 1996; a second (NHER 32621) consisted of six concrete blocks that held iron rails and may have been associated with the coastal battery (see below); a third controlled Paston Road (NHER 39179); a fourth (NHER 39180) Links Road; and a fifth (NHER 39181) the coast road into Mundesley from the west. Associated with these defences were slit trenches and other earthworks (NHER 39147, 39148, 39151, 39182, 39187, 39188, 39189, 39190, 39191, 39192, 39193, 39195, 39196, 39197): although visible on wartime aerial photographs, most have long since disappeared.

The surviving remains of the emergency coastal battery at Mundesley (NHER 14142) are of national importance. The battery, manned by 197 Battery Royal Artillery, was built in 1941. It was armed with two six-inch guns taken from a World War I battleship and mounted on octagonal concrete bases, where the remnants of gun mountings can still be seen. A steel frame overhead was covered with sandbags to protect the gun crews. Magazines for the ammunition and shelters for the crew were in the buried structure that is still visible between the two emplacements. The battery had two powerful searchlights, but these were

Figure 53: The remains of the coastal battery viewed from Trafalgar Court (used with permission)

closer to the cliff edge and their mountings have fallen over the cliff. The two flat roofed structures that housed the generators can be seen a few metres behind the battery. The range finder and command post were to the west, and the Grand Hotel served as an observation post. In the basement there survive two colourful murals which were most probably executed by soldiers stationed there. One portrays a sunken wartime vessel on the seabed surrounded by sea-life. The other is a more allegorical scene of a watery underworld with the devil and his demons wielding tridents among fish, crabs and octopuses. These murals need to be recorded and conserved for the benefit of future generations. When

118

Figure 54: A Second World War mural in the basement of the Grand Hotel showing a sunken vessel (used with permission)

the danger of invasion receded in 1944 the battery was closed and the guns were removed and scrapped in the winter of 1945-46. The site of another possible gun emplacement or earthwork (NHER 39198) is poorly documented and its use is uncertain.

Eight ships of Convoy FS 559 on its way from Newcastle to London were wrecked on Haisborough Sands in the early hours of 6 August 1941. In the wet and stormy weather Happisburgh lighthouse, illuminated for only ten minutes as a convoy was passing, was not visible. An unsubstantiated story is that a German E-boat attack on a passing north-bound convoy caused FS 559 to scatter. Whatever, the section led by the escort trawler *HM Agate* ran aground on the Sands. The ships wrecked were the *SS Oxshott, Afon Towy, Deerwood, Betty Hindley, Aberhill, Gallois[e], Tara* and *HM Agate*. Some internet sites add another vessel, *SS Paddy Hendly*, but Henry Blogg, the famous coxswain of Cromer's lifeboat *H F Bailey*, reported only seven broken-backed cargo vessels on the Sands. Henry Blogg and his crew were decorated for their part in rescuing 137 sailors. Sadly 37 others died including all 16 hands from *HM Agate*.

The cliffs were mined, and once the fear of invasion receded in 1944 mine clearance began. Twenty-six personnel were killed clearing mines on the beaches and cliffs between Yarmouth and Holkham between 1944 and 1953: their memorial near the Watch Tower was unveiled on 2 May 2004. Some civilians were killed when they strayed onto the minefields, including two boys, Roy Riley and Ernest Whitwood, in 1943. The cliffs between Mundesley and Trimingham were so unstable that clearing was halted until 1953. The roadway down to the beach at Trimingham was built so that heavy equipment could be deployed to clear the mines safely. Mines were washed out of the cliffs, and unexploded mines were blown up at 3.00 pm on Fridays: wise householders made sure their windows were open! Alfred Thomas Glew, who drove the armoured bulldozer for twelve years was awarded the British Empire Medal in 1967. The beaches were finally reopened in 1966.

A radar station was established early in 1941 at Trimingham on the site of an earlier beacon and telegraph station which is marked on eighteenth and nineteenth century maps. Initially run by the army, it later became Royal Air Force Trimingham. RAF Mundesley (NHER 38977) which lay south of the Cromer Road was involved in secret radio counter-measures - known as 'beam-bending' - against the radio guidance systems used by raiding German bombers. Later in the war it also operated as a 'splasher' navigational beacon for the USAAF. Its detailed configuration is evident only on aerial photographs, for its site now lies under modern housing. A Royal Observer Corps (ROC) was established in Mundesley in 1934 and served through the war and after. To the west of the parish stands a ROC underground monitoring post (NHER 35420), opened in 1961. It was part of a network of such posts, designed to monitor fallout in the event of a nuclear attack. It closed in 1991.

Figure 55: A Second World War mural of a watery hell from the Grand Hotel (used with permission) - surely worthy of preservation

CONCLUSION

What I have written began as notes to help me and other stewards explain the Museum's collection to visitors and to answer their questions. It has developed a life of its own, but it is still only a foretaste of the riches that may be unearthed by further research into Mundesley's past. There is more work to be done in exploring local and national archives, in recording the memories of local people, in creating a photographic archive, and in safeguarding the character of our historic environment. The footsteps that Mundesley people have made - and are making - on the sands of time are fragile: we need to treasure and preserve them.

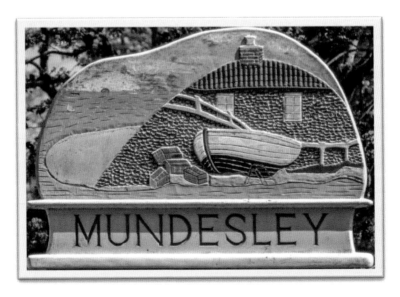

ACKNOWLEDGEMENTS

I am grateful to those who first established and now run Mundesley Museum for preserving much of the parish's heritage that otherwise might have been lost. The Museum's artefacts, records, pictures and photographs have made invaluable contributions to this book.

Many books and articles on Norfolk refer to Mundesley, most often in passing, but I owe particular thanks to the Norfolk Record Society; to the Norfolk and Norwich Archaeological Society; to the on-line Norfolk Historic Environment Record which details many sites and artefacts discovered in the parish; to other websites, especially GENUKI and Wikipedia; to North Norfolk District Council for its *Mundesley Conservation Area Character Appraisal*.

I am grateful for assistance and for permissions to reproduce maps and photographs to the Ordnance Survey; North Norfolk District Council; Norfolk Record Office; Norfolk Local Studies Library; the owners of Trafalgar Court; the owners of Kiln Cliffs Caravan Park; and the Churchwardens of All Saints' Church.

ACKNOWLEDGEMENTS

Many people have contributed to this book. I owe much gratitude to Leigh Caudwell for the excellence of his photography and design. I thank Christopher West for his enthusiasm and energy in driving this project forward and for his researching of some of the illustrations. I owe most to my wife Margaret for her encouragement and forbearance. Any errors that remain are my own.